# PRICKLY PEARS

## Also by Bill Nichols

### HEALTHY FAITH
*A Strategic Plan to Transform Your Head, Heart & Hands*

*Healthy Faith* guides you to develop a faith that works every day in every circumstance. And it gets you what God wants for you—a close, personal relationship with Him, producing a life filled with purpose and peace.

With intellectual integrity, inspirational motivation, and faith-building exercises, *Healthy Faith* provides a practical and comprehensive step-by-step strategy for developing a personal lifestyle plan and a faith that transforms how you think, feel and what you do.

### DEVOTIONS FOR A HEALTHY FAITH
*Get to know God Through His 66 Books*

*Devotions for a Healthy Faith* gives you an opportunity to accept God's invitation to know Him as He reveals Himself to you in His 66 books. Each reading focuses on one book of the Bible, giving you its historical context, information about its writer, and what God is revealing about Himself in the book. Following that is a brief devotional with real-life stories where God discloses His character and His nature in the Bible. The daily devotion closes with two key verses from the book and a few questions for your reflection.

*Devotions for a Healthy Faith* is a helpful book if you are just starting your personal Bible study journey or if you have felt that the Bible is confusing. This sixty-six-day, inspirational book can be used as a private daily devotional guide, a group study guide, or a preaching and teaching resource.

## DIGGING DEEPER
### *Discovering the Original Meaning of the Bible's 30 Key Words*

The Bible is the recorded stories of God's activities in human history, how He reveals Himself, and the ways of living that will make us joyful, peaceful people. Over time, cultural, religious, and political views have changed people's understanding of the original meaning of some of the Bible's key words.

*Digging Deeper* addresses the meanings of thirty of these faith-foundational words. In examining these words from their earliest pictographic forms through the evolution of language and translations, their original God-inspired meanings become clearer.

Designed to be a daily devotional book to inspire, encourage, instruct, and comfort you, *Digging Deeper* is also structured as a resource when you are studying, teaching, or when you are discussing God's Word with others.

# PRICKLY PEARS

*30 DEVOTIONS ON FINDING PEACE, PURPOSE AND HOPE EVEN IN THE MIDST OF YOUR PAIN*

George W. (Bill) Nichols, PhD

*Prickly Pears:*
*30 Devotions on Finding Peace, Purpose and Hope Even in the Midst of Your Pain*

© 2025 by George W. (Bill) Nichols

All rights reserved. No portion of this book may be reproduced, stored in a retrieval system, or transmitted in any form or by any means—electronic, mechanical, photocopy, recording, scanning or other—except for brief quotations, without the prior written permission of the publisher.

Published by GWN Publishing

Scripture quotations marked KJV are taken from the King James Version of the Bible.

Scripture quotations marked MSG are taken from *The Message*, copyright © 1993, 2002, 2018 by Eugene Peterson. Use by permission of NavPress. All rights reserved. Represented by Tyndale House Publishers, Inc.

Scripture quotations marked NIV are taken from *The Holy Bible, New International Version*®, NIV®. Copyright ©1973, 1978, 1984, 2011 by Biblica, Inc. ® Used by permission. All rights reserved worldwide.

Scripture quotations marked NLT are taken from the *Holy Bible, New Living Translation*, copyright © 1996, 2004, 2015 by Tyndale House Foundation. Used by permission of Tyndale House Publishers, Inc., Carol Stream, Illinois 60188. All rights reserved.

ISBN: 979-8-9888854-4-3 (Print)
ISBN: 979-8-9888854-5-0 (eBook)

# TABLE OF CONTENTS

Introduction ............................................................................ xiii
1. Turning Your Mess into Your Message ........................... 1
2. Laughter: A Symptom of the Soul ..................................... 9
3. I Prefer the Neck ................................................................ 15
4. Ants in the Pants of Faith ................................................. 19
5. Patience—The Kind that Works ...................................... 27
6. Diving Deeper .................................................................... 35
7. If you will it, you can do it. Really? ................................ 41
8. Got a burden? Start counting. ......................................... 47
9. Are you one of His sheep? ............................................... 53
10. Are you a ghost flower Christian? ................................ 59
11. Hawks Are Scary … or Not? .......................................... 65
12. The Sparrow Takes Center Stage .................................. 71
13. The Worst Advice I've Ever Heard ............................... 77
14. Can you say it in one line? ............................................. 83
15. Jairus: Turn Your Beliefs into Faith .............................. 89
16. Jairus: Turn Your Pain Into Your Project .................... 95
17. Hard work is the key to success, or is it? .................. 101
18. Stay Connected .............................................................. 107
19. Oh! To Fly Free as a Bird! ............................................. 113
20. Delight in Your Difficulties ......................................... 119
21. He's Watching You ....................................................... 127
22. God-blessed Eyes .......................................................... 133
23. You can get anything if you ask in Jesus's Name! ... 139
24. A Thorn in My Sole ...................................................... 145
25. God's Boomerang Effect .............................................. 151

26. America's Surprising New Epidemic ............................. 159
27. The Not-So-Ordinary Barn Owl ........................................ 167
28. From a Meager Shelter to a Marvelous Mansion ........... 173
29. The Preacher's Coming ..................................................... 181
30. Are you missing the signs while waiting for
the wonders? ............................................................................ 189

About the Author ..................................................................... 197

*Dedication*

*For Phyllis*

By the time you finish reading *Prickly Pears*, you'll understand why I dedicated this book to Phyllis, the love of my life. From helping me recall stories for inclusion to tirelessly correcting my errors, she helped me examine each devotion, making sure it had the practical spiritual value I desired for readers. Finally, in the thorny experiences of my life, my Phyllis has been my encourager, my constant companion, and God's gracious gift to me.

# INTRODUCTION

YOU MAY BE SCRATCHING YOUR HEAD, trying to figure out why I chose *Prickly Pears* as the title for a devotional book. The idea actually came from some life experiences—those prickly, painful times that deepened my faith and softened the outer edges of my soul.

Let me begin by telling you a story. I like peanut butter and jelly on my toast. I mean, I really like it, and I like it every morning. One of my favorite jellies is prickly pear jelly. It's not always possible to find that jelly on the grocery store shelf, and when you do, it is expensive. But I found a source. Kathy worked in the kitchen at a spiritual retreat center that my wife and I visited regularly, and Kathy made all kinds of jellies and jams that we enjoyed while we were there. For several years, I bought prickly pear jelly from Kathy every time we went for a retreat.

I am married to a southern cook who decided she could make prickly pear jelly if Kathy could make it. Phyllis made this decision soon after we moved to the Texas Hill Country where prickly pears grow in abundance. On our walks through the hills around our home, we began to make mental note of the cactuses along our paths, and we watched the blooms morph into fruit. That's when Phyllis began to read all about gathering and cleaning the prickly pears and how to make the jelly.

When in mid-July the prickly pears turned a deep, purplish red, we were prepared. We took off early one morning with two buckets, metal tongs the length of a baseball bat, and dressed in protective clothing: rugged jeans, long-sleeved shirts, and rubber gloves to our elbows. Phyllis warned me that along with the large, visible, spike-like thorns are clusters of almost invisible, tiny hair-like needles called glochids. These glochids go almost unnoticed until they break off in your skin and inflict pain. We were ready for combat with tweezers in my back pocket.

We returned home more than an hour later with two buckets of egg-sized, prickly pear fruits called tunas. Phyllis had also learned that only fire or water would remove the thorns and glochids so that she could handle them to make jelly. Already wearing five extra pounds of July sweat, we had no desire to crank up the grill, stand in the midday

July sun, and singe two buckets of prickly pear fruit, so we chose the ice water bath.

We poured water and dumped ice over the buckets of fruit and let them sit for a while. Then the beating and more sweating started. With the longest handled wooden spoons we had, Phyllis and I stirred and beat those pears like we were human Kitchen-Aid mixers. My job was over at this point.

Phyllis took over with the stock pots of boiling water, cooling, peeling, and mashing the tunas through a cheese cloth-covered strainer to get the coveted, crimson-colored juice. Then came the sugar, slow boiling, and preparing the jars. Hours later, she invited me into the kitchen and introduced me to eight pints of prickly pear jelly and announced that I'd better enjoy them because there would be no more. I can't say that I blame her.

I have often thought about the cost of that goodness and sweetness, and perhaps there are some life lessons the prickly pear has to offer us. These thorny plants grow mainly in the southern states where it is warm and thrive in arid areas where it is more difficult for normal vegetation to survive. They can be found growing in clusters, but sometimes they stand alone in desert lands. Most landowners see them as painful nuisances that need to be removed. However, if you look a little closer you'll see the reasons they have value and are useful.

From ancient times, Native Americans saw the prickly pear cactus as a symbol of resilience, perseverance, and hidden hope. Early archeological discoveries indicate Native Americans ate the prickly pear fruit as part of their diet, relying on them for sustenance and hydration, for medicine, and as a source for needles, containers, and water. They mashed the fruit, boiled it down into prickly pear syrup, juice, or jelly and dried the excess fruit to store for winter. Nutritionists tell us today that these cactuses are rich in vitamins, electrolytes, organic compounds, and minerals.

I have wondered about the first person brave enough to attempt picking and trying to eat a cactus pad or a tuna. With its sharp thorns and tough exterior to protect it, the prickly pear does not look as inviting as a plump peach or a cluster of grapes. But hidden beneath those prickly protectors is a sweet, healthful fruit waiting to be discovered by those willing to explore beneath its unsympathetic surface.

Now you can understand why I look at this thorny fruit as a metaphor for those challenges and trials in our lives, those miseries that cause us such pain. Pain is a common denominator for us humans, and it levels the playing field. We all experience pain in its different forms: physical pain, grief, loss, illness, unhealthy relationships.

If we're but willing to examine our pains and troubles more closely, often we'll find fruitful lessons and blessings God has waiting for us, blessings we'd never know otherwise. The prickly pear cactus, thriving in the desert, is a visual reminder that when you and I are trying to navigate life's wilderness experiences, when we're facing the most difficult obstacles or long-term setbacks in our lives, with God's help, we too possess the remarkable ability to endure and thrive despite all odds.

This idea isn't new. In fact, the Bible is filled with stories of real people who had thorny problems and painful experiences that were transformed into powerful testimonies. Through these real-life stories, we can undoubtedly see the recurring theme of finding sweet, nourishing fruit in the midst of our thorns.

The Apostle Paul is one of the most familiar Bible characters and writers, and he lived with a thorn in his flesh. We do not know what Paul's thorn was, but we know that he prayed repeatedly for God to remove it. Once a fierce and zealous persecutor of Christians, Paul encountered Christ on the road to Damascus and was struck blind—a thorny experience to say the least. The next chapter in his story pictures a transformed Paul. The former persecutor of Christians had become the leader of those whom he had persecuted, a passionate church-planter, a fearless missionary, and a prolific writer of much of the New Testament.

Look at Joseph. His life was clearly filled with prickly pear experiences. He started out as the favored son of a wealthy man, but he was sold into slavery by his own jealous brothers, taken to Egypt by slave-traders, falsely accused by Potiphar's wife, and unfairly thrown into prison. But through those thorny struggles, God helped Joseph stay faithful and find a path to inner peace and purpose. Over time, he rose to become the second most powerful man in Egypt, saving his family and countless lives during a famine.

One of my favorite prickly pear characters is Moses. Talk about a thorny path! Rescued as an infant in a basket, he was brought up as the privileged prince of Egypt's Pharaoh. But after murdering an Egyptian, he fled to the desert only to live with his guilt and confusion. Moses's journey was never smooth, but God had a plan. Moses faced fear, doubt, insecurity, and an impossible-sounding mission to lead God's people out of their Egyptian slavery. Yet, through all of his prickly challenges, Moses experienced God's presence, His protection, and His purpose. He witnessed mighty acts of God: the plagues, the parting of the Red Sea, and God's miraculous provisions as the Israelites journeyed for forty years through the wilderness. And it was to Moses that God gave His Ten Commandments.

Look at Queen Esther. She wasn't born into royalty. Esther started out as a poor Jewish orphan girl. Because of her exceptional beauty, she was taken against her will away from her family and faith to be one of the Persian emperor's many slave concubines. Esther hated it yet was forced to endure shame, pain, and risk. Eventually, the emperor chose her to be his queen. On one occasion, she was faced with an agonizing decision. When her Jewish family was about to be annihilated, she was asked to plead with the king for their lives. By law, approaching the emperor uninvited could mean death. Esther made a courageous but dangerous choice. She confronted her fears to save her people. Her humble decision revealed the sweet fruit of God's blessings, deliverance, and personal dignity.

There are so many more stories of Bible characters who faced pain, suffering, and humiliation, but one I can't leave out is Mary Magdalene. Her tormented past was riddled with all kinds of emotional pain, but her story doesn't end with those thorns. Mary chose to turn from her old ways and follow Christ and is revered as one of our Lord's most loyal and remarkable followers. In fact, God gave her the honor of being one of the first to witness our Lord's resurrection. Her journey from a dark, guilt-ridden past to a forgiven and meaningful life is a testament to the love and power of God.

So, the next time you're feeling the pain of those prickly pear experiences, remember these stories. Think of Paul's persistence, Joseph's resilience, Moses's determination, Esther's bravery, and Mary's transformation. And remember, God used their painful experiences to draw each of them closer to Him and to allow them to see Him at work, but God used their challenges for even greater purposes.

Because of their faith and obedience, God was faithful to use their experiences to bless countless others through history. Here we are, two thousand years later still reading Paul's letters in the New Testament. And look at how God used Joseph, Moses, and Esther to lead and preserve His chosen nation through the centuries: saving them from starvation, from slavery, and from persecution. And what hope Mary Magdalene's story still gives us about Jesus's willingness to forgive us and make it possible for us to have a meaningful life. These men and women changed their focus from their pain to purpose.

Our struggles and challenges may not influence large numbers of people as theirs did, but perhaps through them, we will encounter God in a deeper way, come closer to Him, and be an encouragement or help to just one. For more than a decade, I've been in the metaphorical wilderness, traveling through prickly pear terrain, and I'm still trying to reach beneath the surface of the thorns. I am determined to move my focus from my pain and problems to peace and purpose as these Bible characters did.

Maybe you're still scratching your heads wondering what do prickly pears have to do with me, and how can this devotional book help me? Since all of us are likely to live with thorns that we cannot remove and conditions that keep pushing us down, we need a new way of thinking about our problems and a change in our assumptions about our pain. I wrote this devotional book specifically to be an encouragement and challenge to people like you and me, people who live with prickly pears and want to live a life of peace, purpose, and hope even in the midst of their pain. As I have been and still am traveling my journey with pain and new limitations, I've learned some new and helpful lessons that work for me, lessons that I wish I had known years ago.

You would think by now I would have already figured it all out since I was a former seminary professor, counselor, hospital chaplain, and pastor. For decades I taught the subject and tried my best to minister to people living in painful situations, sympathizing and empathizing with them. But I was at a safe distance with mainly academic or second-hand knowledge as I had studied, taught, and even written books and articles about suffering. That kind of *knowing from a distance* is not the same as the kind that comes from *knowing from a closeup personal experience* with pain. For the first time, my heart was opened to a different kind knowledge about dealing with pain. As I'm sure you can understand, my *knowing* has radically changed.

Twelve years ago, my knowledge of pain and suffering became deeply personal. During these last years, it has seemed that everywhere I turned, I ran into more painful thorns. Some were just uncomfortable, but others were extremely painful and depressing. Some were short-lived. Others seemed like they would never end.

For most of my life, I had been a healthy, athletic fellow. Except for a few bumps, bruises, and breaks, I hardly ever thought much about pain.

My thinking began to change in 2012 when I was diagnosed with prostate cancer. After surgery and all that goes with it, the outcome was good, and life moved on. Then in 2018, a different kind of cancer appeared when the doctor discovered a malignant tumor in my kidney. I underwent months of chemotherapy before the removal of the kidney. I had not completely recovered when another tumor was discovered in my chest, that turned out to be a new form of cancer, a blood cancer. This required weeks of daily radiation treatments. A year later, a stroke surprised me, and before I recovered from that, the shingles struck me on the left side of my face and eye. Shingles were the most painful of all. And two months later, my oncologist diagnosed yet another cancer—an incurable blood cancer, multiple myeloma, which required seven months of additional chemo treatments. Much of this occurred in the midst of the pandemic. As of this writing, I am in temporary remission, as there is no cure. But I'm still dealing with the after-effects of my stroke, treatments, and all the rest.

    Honestly, at times I have felt a bit like Job, like I couldn't get a break. The question for me at that point was no longer *if*, but *what*? What was I going to do with all this unwelcome and unexpected pain? Unlike Job whose friends were discouragers and whose wife told him to curse God and die, I was blessed with family and friends who encouraged me in my faith. I had excellent medical care, and I had the best care a man could have from my best friend, my precious Phyllis, who has been with me every hour of every day including every hospital stay, every treatment, and months and years of recovery. Through these blessings, I began to taste some of the sweetness in the prickly fruit that our Lord had waiting all along for me to discover beneath the thorns.

The sweetest fruit of all was our Lord's presence. Whether it was on the darkest night when I wasn't sure I'd see another sunrise, or when I longed for relief from my discomfort, or when I was surrounded by tenderhearted smiling nurses as I rang the bell signifying my treatment was over, God was present. I could never have experienced Him in such palpable ways had I not experienced the suffering. I have tasted our Lord's love and faithfulness, and I have learned some helpful lessons from Him with every thorn.

I'm still working at practicing those valuable lessons. Lessons like finding ways to use my pain to help me be a more compassionate encourager to fellow sufferers. Lessons like finding something for which to be thankful in every situation and learning that my gratitude was the key that surprisingly opened the door to my path to peace and joy. Lessons like using my thorn in the flesh to remind me of accepting some new rules and boundaries I've discovered I need to live by. Lessons like turning my pain and fatigue into my companion instead of my enemy since it is likely to be with me permanently.

These shifts in thinking helped me to stop being so obsessively preoccupied with my pain and stop expecting to be pain-free. I no longer believe our culture's lie that being pain-free is my only hope for peace and joy. I've found that's just not the truth. I know now that my life does not have to be pain-free to experience joy, purpose, and peace beneath my pain.

Although I've been a Bible teacher almost all of my life, I did not write this book primarily to teach you. It's not a how-to book or a list of biblical steps to educate you on how to overcome your problems and pain. It's a collection of true-life stories from people who have inspired me, stories from my childhood, and others through my *prickly pear journey*. Stories that taught me some valuable lessons—stories like the time a cactus thorn went all the way through my shoe and foot, or the day Phyllis and I witnessed a hawk flying with a hummingbird in his tail-wind, or my experience diving for sunken ships and their treasures.

Each devotional was written with you in mind, with my prayer that it will encourage, comfort, and maybe inspire you to experience the same kind of shift in thinking I've had about my suffering. Maybe you're like the cactus, struggling to live in a desert-like experience. Maybe you're in a relationship where there are sharp thorns and those hard to see glochids with every turn and conversation. Maybe you feel like Job with your own crises coming one after the other. You can't avoid the pain, and you want to know how to deal with it and make sense of it.

I pray this book may move you into a new way of dealing with all you are going through. Remember, Phyllis and I prepared ourselves by getting some good equipment before gathering prickly pears. Hopefully, your new way of thinking about the pain and prickles in your life will prepare you for dealing with them. Just as the inner part of the prickly pear's fruit is a surprising reward for those willing to adjust to its sharp exterior, so too are the blessings of finding God's *more* for those who persevere through their personal trials.

When life hurts, I encourage you to look to see what God is up to and look for His purpose in all of it. Trusting Him will reveal truths that will give meaning to your suffering. It did for me. Recall the valued lesson of the prickly pear: there is sweetness to be found, even in the midst of your pain.

The Apostle Paul gives us the key. "Rejoice in our confident hope. Be patient in trouble, and keep on praying" (Romans 12:12 NLT).

Your fellow sojourner,<br>Bill

# 1. TURNING YOUR MESS INTO YOUR MESSAGE

HAVE YOU EVER HEARD SOMEONE SAY, "Everything that happens is God's will?" That's usually followed by, "Your problem is that you just don't understand right now why it's happening, but you will later." The truth is that not everything that happens to us is God's will or what God would have chosen for us. But even then, God is still involved.

Life can get rough and confusing, but never forget this: You are His beloved child. As your Heavenly Father, He feels your pain, and He only wants the best for you. No matter how tough things get, He can help you turn the situation into something good.

This old saying may sound like a religious platitude, but I found it to be true about the toughest times in my life. Your test can become your testimony. Your mess can become your message. That's the heart of it. The hard times, trials, and tests you face, when handled with the attitude of your Lord, can turn into compelling stories of His love and can show to all those around you the genuineness of your faith.

He had been in the hospital for three rough weeks. It was the last, painful month of my best friend Frank Short's battle with cancer. It had been a harsh journey. His room was a constant flow of nurses and doctors, tending to his needs and his pain. Although the cancer had broken down his body, Frank never let it break his spirit. He always had his signature smile and kind words for those giving care to him. More than one nurse had said to me, "In spite of all his suffering, I believe he's the most cheerful guy I've ever seen."

Right near the end, I overheard one nurse ask him, "With everything you're going through, how do you stay so positive?" I'll never forget his answer, and I can imagine the nurse will remember it too. Frank said, "This cancer may kill me, but it'll never get me down. Whether I'm healed or taken home, I will praise Him." Frank turned his suffering into a powerful testimony.

Not always, but sometimes, our suffering, our miseries, and our messes are tests that give us opportunity to show who we really are and what we really believe. The Bible says, "Dear friends, don't be surprised at the fiery trials you are going through, as if something strange were happening to you. Instead, be very glad—for these trials make you partners with Christ in his suffering, so that you will have the wonderful joy of seeing his glory when it is revealed to all the world" (1 Peter 4:12-13 NLT).

Our Lord does not want us to waste our pain, sorrows, and messy troubles. He wants us to use them for some greater purpose. Do you see your suffering as just a fluke of nature? Is it a consequence of your actions, or did someone else cause it? Or could it be a test? Let's be honest. Most of the time, we can't figure out why these things happen to us. But with God's help, we can always figure out a way to use our problems for a higher purpose.

When I think about Frank, I remember his unwavering faith even in the face of something as terrifying as cancer. He never asked the hard questions: Why? Why me? His response was, "Should I not suffer? Is a servant better than His master?" Frank chose to use his suffering as a platform to praise God, to show others that no matter how dire his circumstances, his faith would remain unshaken. It wasn't just about enduring pain; it was about demonstrating his faith.

And that's something we all can do. It's not easy. Truth is, sometimes it feels downright impossible. But when we lean on God's indwelling Spirit to strengthen us, when we trust that He's with us through the fire, it is possible to turn our tests into testimonies. It's about showing the world that even in our darkest hours, we followers of Jesus believe in His goodness, His abiding presence, and His wisdom in every situation, no matter its difficulty.

Maybe during this time in your life, you or someone you love is dealing with a job loss, a broken relationship, a serious illness, or some other hardship. During those times, it's normal and human for all of us to feel lost, to question, and to struggle. But in those moments, remember you're not alone. God is with you. And He can use your pain or your confusion to bring about something beautiful and helpful. He can use your response to inspire others and to bring hope to those who are watching.

It's your choice as to what you will do with your difficulties. But, if you choose to trust your Heavenly Father, He can and will use any difficult situation you go through to strengthen your spirit, comfort your heart, or maybe inspire others. The Bible word for *test* actually comes from a word that means to examine closely or to take a close look. So, if you or a loved one is going through a tough time, it is your choice: will you take charge of your situation and make the decision to make today's test tomorrow's witness?

So, even when it doesn't make sense to some, let's choose to thank Him and trust Him, even when it hurts. With God's help, let's choose to turn our mess into a message and our tests into testimonies. And who knows? Maybe one day, someone will remember your journey and find the strength they need to keep going. Maybe your testimony will be the light they need in their darkest hour.

## FROM GOD'S WORD

We can rejoice, too, when we run into problems and trials, for we know that they help us develop endurance. And endurance develops strength of character, and character strengthens our confident hope of salvation. And this hope will not lead to disappointment. For we know how dearly God loves us, because he has given us the Holy Spirit to fill our hearts with his love.

(Romans 5:3-5 NLT)

For our present troubles are small and won't last very long. Yet they produce for us a glory that vastly outweighs them and will last forever! So we don't look at the troubles we can see now; rather, we fix our gaze on things that cannot be seen. For the things we see now will soon be gone, but the things we cannot see will last forever.

(2 Corinthians 4:17-19 NLT)

Dear brothers and sisters, when troubles of any kind come your way, consider it an opportunity for great joy. For you know that when your faith is tested, your endurance has a chance to grow.

(James 1:2-3 NLT)

So be truly glad. There is wonderful joy ahead, even though you must endure many trials for a little while. These trials will show that your faith is genuine. It is being tested as fire tests and purifies gold—though your faith is far more precious than mere gold. So when your faith remains strong through many trials, it will bring you much praise and glory and honor on the day when Jesus Christ is revealed to the whole world.

(1 Peter 1:6-7 NLT)

**YOUR PRAYER**

Dear Father, I must confess, sometimes painful things and messy things in my life do feel impossible for me to handle. So, I ask You to help me lean on Your indwelling Spirit to strengthen me and make it possible to turn my tests into testimonies for Your glory. Thank You for Your goodness, abiding presence, and wisdom in every situation in my life. AMEN.

## 2. LAUGHTER: A SYMPTOM OF THE SOUL

DO YOU LAUGH A LOT? Maybe your laugh is like my dad's, a quiet chuckle inside. Or maybe it's one of those contagious, full body laughs that gets everybody in the room laughing. I've heard it said that laughter is a symptom of your soul.

If that's true, and I think it is, checking out your laughter-gauge could be a good way to help determine your soul's health. I'm talking about the level of your soul's joy in times that could make you sad. Are you peaceful on dark days? What's the expression on your face when life keeps smacking you around?

Maybe it would be best for us to think of this laughter-gauge as a blood pressure cuff we wrap around our souls to check out our joy level. I say joy level because our happiness level is determined by our circumstances, whereas our level of joy is determined by what's inside us.

Pause for a minute right now and put a spiritual stethoscope to your soul and let's see how your joy and peace levels are doing. Listen closely and see if you can tell how your soul is answering questions like these.

- Do I feel like sad and down most of the time?
- Am I laughing less these days?
- Lately, do I see problems everywhere I look?
- When I wake up in the morning, would I rather just stay in bed?
- Do I usually prefer being alone more than being around others?
- Most of the time, do I feel dissatisfied with everything and everyone?

If you answered yes to more than a two of these questions, your soul's health is needing some heavy doses of joy and peace. The Apostle Paul writes about one of those times when he was in a discouraging situation. He was alone, in chains, in a Roman dungeon, and there was seemingly no way out. He wrote his Christian friends to let them know how he was doing on the inside in spite of his dire circumstances.

"I'm glad in God, far happier than you would ever guess—happy that you're again showing such strong concern for me. Not that you ever quit praying and thinking about me. You just had no chance to show it. Actually, I don't have a sense of needing anything personally. I've learned by now to be quite content (at peace with) whatever my circumstances. I'm just as happy with little as with much, with much as with little. I've found the recipe for being happy whether full or hungry, hands full or hands empty. Whatever I have, wherever I am, I can make it through anything in the One (Jesus) who makes me who I am" (Philippians 4:11-14 MSG).

My friend, Bill Zehner, was a smart, middle-aged gentleman, who worked as the CFO of our company. Being buried in numbers all day, every day, you wouldn't think he would be such a happy, light-hearted fellow. But he was.

I'll never forget what Zehner said just days before he died. He had endured a long series of different cancer treatments and their life-depriving side effects for several months. His oncologist was searching for some medication that would slow down his rapidly spreading cancer diagnosed as terminal.

Weak and worn, Bill came by the office one morning, and everyone gathered to greet him. We all had a sense of what he was facing. After all the hugs, I asked him how he was feeling. He dropped his head and his face took on a serious frown. No one moved in the silent waiting.

Finally, Bill looked up and delivered the grim report that his oncologist was trying a new kind of treatment that included an injection of female hormones. He further explained that the medicine had an unusual side-effect.

It was obvious he was waiting for someone to ask, so I asked out of my concern, "What unusual side-effect, Bill?" He looked down again, and then slowly looked up and said, "Ever since I started taking the female hormones, I have this insatiable desire to go shopping." At first no one knew how to react. Then we got it, and we all broke out into laughter.

That was the Bill Zehner we had all known for a long time—a man of great faith, a man full of joy, and a man full of the peace of God. His joy was not determined by his circumstances but by his trust in his Lord.

Bill lived his life fully with his peace-and-joy-gauge reading *full*. I pray you're doing the same.

## FROM GOD'S WORD

Dear brothers and sisters, when troubles of any kind come your way, consider it an opportunity for great joy. For you know that when your faith is tested, your endurance has a chance to grow. So let it grow, for when your endurance is fully developed, you will be perfect and complete, needing nothing.

(James 1:2-4 NLT)

I have told you these things so that you will be filled with my joy. Yes, your joy will overflow!

(John 15:11 NLT)

I have told you all this so that you may have peace in me. Here on earth, you will have many trials and sorrows. But take heart because I have overcome the world.

(John 16:33 NLT)

## YOUR PRAYER

Father, I admit that sometimes I don't feel happy at all. Things get difficult. And sometimes I get down and feeling sorry for myself. But, as I remember Your sacrificial love for me on the cross, I am filled once again with Your peace and joy. Thank You for always being with me no matter what. AMEN.

## 3. I PREFER THE NECK

"Parents say the weirdest things," I whispered to my older sister, Louise. I had just watched Mama pass up a heaping platter of plump, lip-smacking, golden-crusted Southern fried chicken to pick up a bony, shriveled-up piece that looked like something you'd toss out to a stray cat. It was then Mama made one of those makes-no-sense parent proclamations, "I prefer the neck."

Really? Who prefers a bony chicken neck over a succulent thigh? Years later I understood. Mama didn't really *prefer* the neck. She preferred something more important.

In those days our family of six was so poor that Mama always took less of everything so we kids could have more. It's that Christ-like selflessness that any mother practices when she loves her kids more than herself. It's how selfless, non-self-centered people behave. It was the core characteristic of our Lord, heard in His words, and seen in everything He did.

Selflessness is at the heart of Jesus's Golden Rule, "Do to others as you would like them to do to you" (Luke 6:31 NLT). It's your Savior's main message to you. He penned it in His own blood from the cross. "I loved you so much that I preferred, more than staying safe in heaven, to leave my Father and give up my life for you."

Unbelievers in Jesus's day convinced themselves that Jesus was a lunatic to believe that people could prefer a selfless life. Living selflessly went against everything their self-centered, self-entitled culture taught them. The centuries haven't changed man's basic nature, but Jesus made the difference.

The opposite is true for those of us who take on our Lord's selfless attitude and actions. We have experienced Jesus's strange sounding, unexplainable yet satisfying admonition. The Apostle Paul reminds us, "You should remember the words of the Lord Jesus: 'It is more blessed to give than to receive'" (Acts 20:35 NLT). Giving more and taking less does not seem crazy at all. It works. It surprisingly gives us more than we ever imagined. Being selfless is not only the way to please God, but this humility takes us on a journey to the life we always wanted. The more you become selfless, the more you are able to handle your prickly-pear pains and problems.

After all these years when I am passed a platter of plump, delicious chicken, just before I choose my piece, what do you suppose comes to my mind? Of course, I think of my unselfish, godly Mama. And sometimes, it reminds me of how much Jesus loved me and took less that I might have more.

### FROM GOD'S WORD

He has brought down princes from their thrones and exalted the humble.

(Luke 1:52 NLT)

You should remember the words of the Lord Jesus: "It is more blessed to give than to receive.

(Acts 20:35 NLT)

If you try to hang on to your life, you will lose it. But if you give up your life for my sake, you will save it.

(Luke 9:24 NLT)

### YOUR PRAYER

Father, let me begin by confessing that as I look back over my life, I haven't been an "I-prefer-the-neck" kind of person. Too often, I've been more interested in taking care of my own needs and wants than I have been interested in the needs of others. Thank You for unselfishly giving Your Son to die for me. Help me today that every decision I make will be what Jesus would do. AMEN.

# 4. ANTS IN THE PANTS OF FAITH

I'VE NEVER LIKED NICKNAMES. Usually, they're no more than playground exaggerations of kids' appearances like Chubby, Grumpy, and Shorty. Unfortunately, nicknames commonly catch on and stick for life. When he was in kindergarten, his tall friend gave him the nickname *Shorty*. No one imagined Shorty would become be the 6-foot, 6-inch, 330-pound center on the high school football team. What a misleading nickname!

That's what happened to Thomas. He was one of the most courageous and faithful of Jesus's twelve disciples. Then centuries after the four Gospels were written, an anonymous church historian read Thomas's story and erroneously gave Thomas a most misleading nickname, *Doubting Thomas*. Although the label is not found in the Bible or in any other early Christian document, it became a commonly held interpretation of Thomas's response to the news that Jesus had risen from the dead. (John 20:24-29)

During His last trip to Jerusalem, Jesus's life was threatened by His religious enemies. Later He told His disciples He was returning to Jerusalem because His Father had told Him it was time for His purpose to be fulfilled. Fearing for His life and their own, the disciples begged Him to not go, but Jesus explained that He was compelled to go. All but one of the twelve sat silently in fear.

It was in that moment that Thomas alone boldly stood up and challenged the others with his remarkably courageous words, "Let us also go, that we may die with him" (John 11:16 KJV). Those were not the words of a *Doubting Thomas* but those of a *Seeking Thomas*.

After Jesus's crucifixion, burial, and resurrection, on the third day the news was out that Jesus had risen from the dead and had been seen. All the disciples, except Thomas, were huddled in a small room when Jesus appeared to them, fulfilling what He had told them earlier. Later, when Thomas entered the room and was told that Jesus was alive, he made his now unforgettable confession, "I won't believe it unless I see the nail wounds in his hands, put my fingers into them, and place my hand into the wound in his side" (John 20:25 NLT).

Thomas's words, "I won't believe it unless," were not the cowardly, faithless words of an unbeliever, but the faithful seeking-the-truth words of a longtime believer. He was saying the same thing he heard his Lord say to those who didn't believe He was the Son of God. In essence, Jesus told them not to blindly accept as true the rumors or persuasive words of anyone until they first checked them out. He called for His followers to see for themselves if what was being said could be verified by personal evidence.

In our lives, we often find ourselves in Thomas's shoes, facing situations that shake our faith to the core. We ask God, "Why is this happening to me? Why don't You answer my prayers?" Such questions don't necessarily indicate the lack of our faith, but it can show the depth of our desire to be honest with our Lord and ourselves. Our hesitations do not always signify our decision to stop believing but our dedication to keep seeking to discover what our Lord wants us to do. For those trying to be humble followers, doubting is not the opposite of faith but an essential part of our journey of faith.

It's important to remember that there are three types of doubts, defined by one's motive. *Defensive doubts* are those whose motive is not to find the truth, but to defend one's prejudices. *Destructive doubts* are those whose motive is not to help, but to hurt or tear down. *Discovering doubts* are those whose motive is to discover the truth by examining, seeking, or exploring the evidence.

Unfortunately, in our culture, the word *doubt* is usually equated with being defensive or destructive. So, when we doubt, we tend to feel guilty, or we hide our doubts and try to appear piously confident. But the truth is, handling our doubts in those ways guarantees they will stir up intense and disturbing emotions in us. We will begin to have deep and unexplainable periods of fear, anger, and even depression. Such uncontrolled emotions can make it difficult for us to simply get up and keep going.

However, your doubts don't have to be your enemies. You can choose to think of your doubts as your friends, friends who are reminding you that you are not a bad person who has deserted the Lord, but you are an honest Christ-follower who is seeking to develop a stronger, more resilient faith. You can choose to make your doubt your friendly wake-up service that rouses you and motivates you to get up and exercise your faith.

Frederick Buechner, the highly respected theologian once said, "Doubts are the ants in the pants of faith; they keep faith alive and moving." His quote reminds me of the time when I rushed out to help my neighbor with a water leak in his backyard. Without noticing, I'd sat down next to the leak but right on top of an anthill. As you would imagine, those tiny ants became powerful motivators, stimulating me to quickly jump up and get moving. In the same way, our doubts can stir us from our complacency and push us to get moving toward a more vigorous faith.

Jesus Himself was known more for questioning the accepted norms and beliefs of His time than He was for going along with the majority. C.S. Lewis, the internationally-renowned literary genius and declared atheist, explained that one of the reasons he became a Christian was because of his doubts, not in spite of them. He discovered that questioning and seeking are integral to having an unshakable faith and genuine relationship with God.

In moments of pain and uncertainty, we all know that doubting can add to our agony and insecurity about our relationship with the Lord. But it is precisely in these times that our faith is refined and strengthened the most.

I encourage you to join *Seeking Thomas* and your many fellow Christ-followers who throughout history have been remembered for being great heroes and heroines of faith. But they were also great questioners and doubters too. Let's never forget, where there is no questioning, there is no real faith, for the essence of faith is risking, depending, trusting in something or someone outside ourselves.

Each day, as you seek to deal with your own prickly pears, your difficult circumstances, your painful problems, I pray you will make that Christ-like decision to do as Thomas did—embrace your doubts, not as deterrents to your faith but as ants in your pants of your faith.

## FROM GOD'S WORD

Consider it a sheer gift, friends, when tests and challenges come at you from all sides. You know that under pressure, your faith-life is forced into the open and shows its true colors. So don't try to get out of anything prematurely. Let it do its work so you become mature and well-developed, not deficient in any way.

(James 1:2-4 MSG)

Dear friends, do not believe everyone who claims to speak by the Spirit. You must test them to see if the spirit they have comes from God. For there are many false prophets in the world.

(1 John 4:1 NLT)

Examine yourselves to see if your faith is genuine. Test yourselves.

(2 Corinthians 13:5 NLT)

## YOUR PRAYER

Dear Father, as I honestly look over my past and how I've made decisions, I am ashamed that I have not given much thought to engaging my faith in all I do. Sometimes when I look at all that's going on around me, I question Your judgement and Your love. I am so sorry for being so very prideful and foolish. I know I don't deserve it, but please forgive me, Father. By Your grace, kindly use my times of doubting and questioning as opportunities to help me grow in spiritual strength and closeness to You. Help me be more like You in how I respond to all of my difficulties and questions. I sincerely want to please You, Lord. AMEN.

## 5. PATIENCE—THE KIND THAT WORKS

"THE KEY TO EVERYTHING IS PATIENCE." Quite a bold statement, isn't it? Some say this quote by Arnold Glasow is the most famous ever written on patience. I'm not sure if that is true, but I am certain that our heavenly Father considers patience one of His four greatest virtues—love, joy, peace, and patience. (Galatians 5:22-23 NLT)

Patience may not be the key to everything, but it's critical to maintaining your love, joy, and peace. Any time these primary values come under attack by life's problems, they are torn apart without patience. Patience is the spiritual glue that makes it possible for us to stand firm under any threat.

Since patience is so important to our Lord and to our everyday lives, we need to understand exactly what it is. Patience is having an inner peace, an unshakable calmness, and secure stability, even during the worst of circumstances.

Patience makes even the weakest of us able to be joyful, hopeful, peaceful, and even thankful despite suffering, loss, aggravating people, or any other type of trouble. And it's doing so without getting angry, upset, or depressed.

The original root Hebrew word for patience is *hupomeno* which comes from the combination of two words, *hupo* and *meno*. *Hupo* means under, and *meno* means to stand firmly. Put them together, they mean to be able to stand firmly under any storm. If we have patience, we are able to be stable under any assault.

However, be careful. There are two very different kinds of patience. The first kind is self-made and self-sustained. It depends solely on you, on your brain talking to the emotional and physical parts of your *self*.

You can use self-care techniques like meditation, self-hypnosis, deep breathing, and others. Can such self-controlled ways of increasing your patience do any good? Sure, they will. Should you use them? Sure, you should. Use all the tools God makes available to you. But keep in mind, this self-care way has its limitations. I call it the *grin and bear it* way. It comfortably fits right in with our relatively new digital culture. Everything around us has become faster, simpler, and more convenient.

Currently, if you feel hungry, you don't have to go through the painstaking process of preparing food and washing dishes. Just tap your phone a few times, and your food is delivered within minutes. And there are no dishes to wash.

In our day, we expect instant gratification. Regrettably, we've started viewing patience as a weakness. When a storm comes, we say to ourselves, *grin and bear it*. Patience means, "Hang in there. Don't worry. Everything will be fine in short time." For many, patience simply means not losing your temper or not getting antsy when waiting.

A recent University of California study found that a simple grin can significantly reduce pain. They seemed to conclude that the secret to handling any problem was to fake it 'til you make it.

The idea is to trick your brain: Simply grin and pretend. The fancy name for this psycho-spin is facial feedback hypothesis. This positive thinking way works some. But when we face more serious situations like a severe sickness, a dysfunctional or dying relationship, or a dying body, the *grin and bear it* way isn't enough. It can be helpful, but not sustainable.

I was bombarded by a barrage of physical and emotional problems: a car accident that nearly took my life, the deaths of my parents, three bouts with unexpected life-threatening cancers. Those problems convinced me that the old self-produced, *grin and bear it* way was not, and never would work. There had to be a better way.

The second kind of patience is what I like to call the *thank-and-trust-Him* kind of patience. It's patience that works both short-term and long-term. It worked for Jesus, and it has worked for me and millions of Christians for centuries.

The more I studied the Jesus-way of handling His pain, sorrow, and grief, even His unimaginable suffering before and during His crucifixion, the clearer it became. Jesus's kind of patience worked for Him. His way was not a *grin and bear* it kind of patience, but a *thank and trust Him* patience. His way was to choose to continually tell His Father how He trusted Him and how thankful He was for His Father's love, inner peace, presence, and provisions through everything. Jesus's way was to focus on God's provisions, not His own problems.

Paul followed Jesus's example when he said, "I quit focusing on the handicap and began appreciating the gift. It was a case of Christ's strength moving in on my weakness. Now I take limitations in stride, and with good cheer, these limitations that cut me down to size—abuse, accidents, opposition, bad breaks. I just let Christ take over! And so the weaker I get, the stronger I become" (2 Corinthians 12:9 MSG).

You might be saying, "I would be more patient, but you don't understand what I'm going through. If you did, you'd understand why I don't have much patience."

You're right. I don't know what you're going through. But I do know this: patience does not come easy.

Like you, I've had my struggles: three kinds of life-threatening cancers, multiple chemotherapies, bouts of radiation, a stroke, painful neuropathy, endless trips to the hospital and doctors' offices. So, I empathize with you.

But what I've learned through it all is that our Lord's kind of peaceful patience is radically different from our self-made, grit-your-teeth, and just hold-on-the-best-you-can kind of patience. His thank-and-trust-Him way has worked, and it's worked amazingly. It's made all the difference in my life when I realized it was a gift of God and it's like faith because it requires trusting. His patience took over when I let go and let Him take over through every part of my *self*.

I don't know what hardships you or your loved ones are going through right now. But I do know this. Our Heavenly Father wants you to have His special kind of patience. But remember, patience that works is a choice. Which way will you choose?

### FROM GOD'S WORD

Wait patiently for the Lord. Be brave and courageous. Yes, wait patiently for the Lord.

(Psalm 27:14 NLT)

Whoever is patient has great understanding, but one who is quick-tempered displays folly.

(Proverbs 14:29 NIV)

Rejoice in our confident hope. Be patient in trouble, and keep on praying.

(Romans 12:12 NLT)

### YOUR PRAYER

Dear Father, I am humbled and deeply grateful for Your patience with me. I confess I have let You down so many times. I've been so impatient, so self-centered. I'm sorry I've disappointed You. Please forgive me. Above everything, I want to please You. I do love You with all my heart and want to show You by trusting and thanking You no matter what happens. Help me, Father, to follow Jesus's example. AMEN.

## 6. DIVING DEEPER

DID YOU KNOW THERE ARE OVER 5,000 shipwrecks along the southeast Florida coastline? Those sunken ships bring treasure hunters from across the globe all searching for caches of silver, gold, and jewels. As a scuba diver and Bible reader, I couldn't help but see some noticeable parallels between these buried vessels and diving deeper into the Word of God.

Growing up near those same beautiful Florida beaches, I spent countless hours snorkeling in the topaz blue waters. Little did I know as a young boy that beneath the surface lay wooden hulls of sunken ships loaded with treasures. I learned that centuries earlier Spanish explorers extracted silver, gold, and precious gems from the mountains of Mexico and South America. As they embarked on their journeys back to Spain, they attempted to navigate around Florida's perilous coral reefs. Unfortunately, storms and hurricanes often caused them to crash into the reefs and join the infamous graveyard of Florida shipwrecks.

Fast forward a few hundred years, and these misfortunes became the motivation for scuba divers to become fortune hunters. Intrigued by their discoveries, I too caught the treasure-hunters' bug.

I remember the day I read about scuba divers unearthing a 300-year-old shipwreck not far from the beach where I regularly snorkeled. The treasures they found were valued at over $500,000. That moment marked a turning point for me. I decided to leave behind my shallow-water snorkel gear and invest in some deep-water scuba equipment. It was expensive for me, but I was willing to pay for it because I was obsessed with the prospect of unearthing millions of dollars of hidden riches.

My deep-water scuba diving experiences did open up a whole new world to me, a world of sea life I had never seen and sounds I had never even imagined. There is nothing quite like the ethereal quiet and serenity when diving in the deep water. It's odd and interesting that sound travels four times faster underwater even though water is a denser medium than air. So, what you hear in the deep is so different and almost impossible to tell the direction or the nearness of what is making the sound.

Reflecting on those early dives, I couldn't help but think about some obvious similarities between them and when I began to dive deeper into the riches of God's Word. Just as my enjoyment kept growing for exploring the ocean's depths, mysteriously my hunger kept growing for diving deeper into the Scriptures to discover God's treasures. Learning to pause and meditate on His word and listen to His inaudible voice were more rewarding than I could have ever imagined.

Just as the shipwrecks off the Florida coast hold fascinating stories of the past, the Bible holds true-life stories and timeless truths that can transform our lives. But we must be willing to dive deep, to let go of our shallow-water devotions, and plunge into the depths of our Lord's storybook.

I had to invest in some expensive scuba gear to even have a chance at finding treasure, and I had to make some costly decisions when I began plunging more deeply into God's Word. I had to invest time, changing my priorities and schedule to give my Father's Word its rightful place. If you want to diver deeper, you will need to make the same investment of your time, and you will need to invest in some necessary study tools. I suggest a Bible dictionary, a commentary, and at least two recognized modern translations of the Bible. I prefer translations like these: *The New Living Translation* (my favorite), or *The New International Version*, or *The Bible in Contemporary Language* (commonly called *The Message*). It also means establishing a consistent daily discipline. The investment seems substantial at first, but you'll discover that the rewards are immeasurable.

Just as deep-sea divers must plunge into the ocean's unknown depths to find the really good stuff, we too must immerse ourselves in the depths of his Word to find our Lord's priceless gifts. Within its pages lie countless spiritual gems just waiting for us to discover, enjoy, and feast upon. Each verse and often each Word, like precious jewels, offers unmatched spiritual wisdom, guidance, and inspiration you will not find anywhere else.

I imagine you're wondering if I ever discovered any shipwrecks with gold, silver, or precious jewels. No. I only explored the disintegrated pieces of a ship and found a cannonball. But when I dove into God's Word, I did discover treasures that were worth far more than any earthly fortune. I pray you will join me in diving deep into the ocean of His Word and pausing to meditate on each of His gems. As you do, I promise, you will find treasures that last for eternity. And as a bonus, you'll receive not only your Father's treasures, but something even more precious—a closer relationship with the Treasure Maker.

Will you join me today and stop skimming the surface and dive deeper?

## FROM GOD'S WORD

In him lie hidden all the treasures of wisdom and knowledge.

(Colossians 2:3 NLT)

Where your treasure is, there will your heart be also.

(Matthew 6:21 KJV)

Cry out for insight, and ask for understanding. Search for them as you would for silver; seek them like hidden treasures. Then you will understand what it means to fear the Lord, and you will gain knowledge of God.

(Proverbs 2:3-5 NLT)

## YOUR PRAYER

Dear Father, please forgive me for giving my heart to less valuable things. I've been immersing my mind and heart in the treasures that leave me unsatisfied and don't last. You gave me Your all, but I confess I've only been giving You a mere token of my attention. Help me, Lord. I sincerely want to dive deep in Your word and hear Your voice, Your truth, and Your promises. Draw me closer to You as I meditate on Your word. AMEN.

## 7. IF YOU WILL IT, YOU CAN DO IT. REALLY?

THIS MORNING, I'VE BEEN THINKING ABOUT YOU. Not you personally, but about the hundreds of people like you. Over the decades, as their pastor, counselor, or hospital chaplain, people have come to me with their personal problems like the ones you might be dealing with right now.

Over the years, I tried to do my best to provide hurting folks with sound, helpful advice that worked. Lately, I've been thinking back over what people have said helped them the most. Maybe some of what they've told me could be of some help to you in your situation.

I've come to realize that we are all more alike than we are different. You may be dealing with a broken heart or heart attack, a life-threatening disease or an unhealthy relationship, or some uncontrollable addiction, or something completely different. But I do know this, we all eventually have to deal with painful problems and desire to overcome them.

There are two other things I know about you. First, dealing with your problem is psychologically painful. Second, you CAN get through this, and you CAN get on top of it. But it will take more than time and your willpower. As important and powerful as willpower is, it's not all-powerful. One of our most self-deceptive, self-destructive, and yet widespread popular sayings is, "You can do anything if you put your mind to it." Some put it this way, "If you will it, you can do it." Really?

Thinking back over years of listening to people who could not overcome their problems no matter how much they willed it, I can hear them shout in unison in response to those catchy but misleading sayings: "No, you can't. Will it all you want, you will never be able to do it on your own."

For some, a relentless willpower works in dealing with the easy stuff in their lives, but it never works for long when it comes to handling the most important issues of our lives. It's never enough for dealing with things like relationships, love, forgiveness, feeling safe, having inner peace, facing losses, death, and eternity. In those areas, we need more than our willpower has to offer.

This is why the highly successful Alcoholics Anonymous (AA) 12-step program begins with its critically important, Bible-based profession: "We admitted we were powerless over alcohol—that our lives had become unmanageable." AA participants are unanimous in affirming that this first admission-step is crucial in overcoming and managing any kind of addiction or harmful habit.

I'll call her Sofia. She was a financially successful, middle-aged woman who managed a team of pharmaceutical salespeople. She was a powerful, take-control-woman with an addiction that controlled her. When Sofia came for counseling, I advised her to join a faith-based support group. With the guidance of her group and her newfound reliance on God, Sofia started seeing real changes.

Actually, I could exchange Sofia's name and a few other details in her story, and it would be the story of too many people that I have counseled. More importantly, it tells the one truth that I believe our Lord wants us to remember as we're struggling with our own challenges. Willpower and our best efforts are extremely helpful, but they do not come near the effectiveness of partnering with our Lord's power. Paul reminded us of the Lord's words to him about partnering with His grace and power when Paul was at his weakest, "My grace is sufficient for you, for my power is made perfect in weakness" (2 Corinthians 12:9 NIV).

This doesn't mean we should lazily do nothing and leave it all up to God. That's never been our

Father's way. He does not want us to stop setting goals and working hard. He wants us to admit our limitations, to recognize that our minds, hearts, and abilities are all His gifts, and to invite Him to guide us and work in us and through us.

The Bible provides numerous examples of individuals who overcame great obstacles not by trying to fly solo, but through partnering with our all-powerful, all-knowing God. Think of David, who defeated Goliath not by his own willpower and strength, but because he trusted in God to use his abilities (1 Samuel 17:45-47). Or think about Moses who led the Israelites out of Egypt and through the Red Sea by relying on God's guidance (Exodus 3:11-12).

Robert Frost, an American poet, says, "The best way out is always through." But we can be grateful that we don't have to endure and go *through* alone. Don't fall for our culture's destructive lie that you can do anything you put your mind to. Many wounded, weary, and disappointed followers have fallen by the wayside trying to overcome life's problems alone. I pray that you won't be one of those. Instead embrace Jesus's wise counsel that all is possible with God our Father.

## FROM GOD'S WORD

With man this is impossible, but with God all things are possible.

(Matthew 19:26 NLT)

Don't copy the behavior and customs of this world, but let God transform you into a new person by changing the way you think. Then you will learn to know God's will for you, which is good and pleasing and perfect.

(Romans 12:2 NLT)

The LORD is my strength and my shield; / my heart trusts in him, and he helps me. / My heart leaps for joy, / and with my song I praise him.

(Psalm 28:7 NIV)

But those who hope in the LORD / will renew their strength. / They will soar on wings like eagles; / they will run and not grow weary, / they will walk and not be faint.

(Isaiah 40:31 NIV)

## YOUR PRAYER

Dear Father, I want to begin by asking Your forgiveness for living most of my life the way the world does. I've tried to do things by my own willpower and my own strength. Because so much of what I've accomplished seemed to prove that I could handle most things on my own, I deceived myself by believing that worldly lie. Over time, I've discovered it the hard way that I cannot handle the most important things alone. I'm totally incapable. I need You. Help me, my Lord, to trust You, follow You, depend on You to use every part of me to serve You. In Jesus's name I pray. AMEN.

## 8. GOT A BURDEN? START COUNTING.

I GREW UP POOR. But, at the time, I didn't know it. As I look back now, we were the poorest family in our neighborhood of Pompano Beach, Florida. Presently, Pompano Beach is a highly-populated, swanky, resort city darted with high-rise ocean-front hotels and condominiums. But in those days, it was no more than a trashy, seaside fishing village with a population of 2,233.

Our family of six lived in a rickety old rent house that leaned to one side. It looked like it might fall over, but it never did. Daddy said it must have been built of good stuff since it was still standing after nearly one hundred years, even after being beat up annually by Florida coastal hurricanes.

I'm sure you've seen a house like ours every time you've driven through that part of most any town where the poorest folks live. It's the kind of place that causes passersby to nod their heads while thinking it was an eyesore. Rotten boards needed replacing. The sun bleached, raw wood exterior thirsted for a fresh coat of paint, and the leaks in the roof needed repairing.

The owner was always going to get around to the repairs, but in the meantime, we were left to deal with the issues. A leaky roof and Florida rains are not a good combination. Lucky me, none of the leaks were in my bedroom. My sisters had all the fun of putting out buckets.

I knew our house was not perfect. But I loved that ramshackle old house. It was home, the only one I'd ever had. Maybe it did shout, "These people are poor." But I was totally unaware of it. Nobody ever said to me, "You're poor."

We didn't have a car. Daddy's company loaned us one. We didn't have store bought clothes. Mama made them. We didn't have a TV or other things we consider necessities now. But, growing up, I was a happy, contented skinny, little guy.

I had my own dream of a playground of untouched, wooded acreage where my buddies and I climbed trees and searched for buried treasure. I had the best meals a kid could want. Daddy worked at the farmer's market, and nearly every night he brought home a basket of the freshest vegetables imaginable. I had two super sisters who made me feel like I was the best brother in the world. I can assure you; I was not. And best of all, I had two parents who continually told me how much they loved me and showed me in more ways than I can count.

Poor? Not me. That never crossed my mind. Until that night.

It was bill-paying time. Mama and Daddy were huddled around the kitchen table shuffling a stack of bills. I overheard Mama say, "George, we don't have enough to pay all of them. Which ones do you think we can put off for a while? Thank the Lord for the blessing of my new babysitting job. Won't be long before we'll be able to catch up on all of these bills."

Suddenly, for the first time in my short life, I realized we couldn't pay our bills. We were poor. I watched as they smiled at each other, hugged, gathered up all their bill-paying stuff, and went about their nightly routine as if nothing was problematic. Daddy strolled off to the living room to listen to the evening baseball game on the radio. As usual, Mama went to the kitchen to prepare sandwiches for tomorrow's school lunch boxes.

When I slowly moseyed up behind Mama at the counter, I recognized she was doing what she always did. She was humming her favorite chorus.

*"Count your blessings, name them one by one,*
*Count your many blessings, see what God has done.*

*Count your blessings, name them one by one,*
*And it will surprise you what the Lord has done."*

Seems like she softly sang that chorus to herself every time she had some new prickly-pear life experience. But that night I asked Mama, "How can you be singing about blessings when you and Daddy don't have enough money to pay our bills?" After many decades, I've never forgotten Mama's answer. She stopped what she was doing, looked at me, and said, "Bill, that's exactly when you most need to count your blessings. When you feel you don't have enough! Enough money. Enough strength. Enough courage. Enough whatever. Anytime you have a burden, immediately start counting. You'll be surprised how many, many, more blessings you have than burdens."

For years now, I've put it to the test. When the burden of grief came from the loss of my life-long friend who died of cancer, when my pain from a head-on car accident seemed unbearable, and with three cancer diagnoses of my own, Mama's count-your-blessings way has proven true every time.

I can't explain it. But something supernatural and comforting happens to you when you look a burden straight in the face and start remembering all that God is doing for you. You begin to realize how really rich you are. You begin thanking God more for what you have rather than complaining about what you don't have.

I eventually realized what I thought was Mama's count-your-blessings way is God's way. It's the spiritual way. The Jesus way. The poor-in-spirit way. Jesus said, "Blessed are the poor in spirit." I believe you could correctly say it this way, "If you're poor in spirit, count your many blessings. Humbly thank God for how truly rich you are, and He will bless you even more."

So where is your focus today? On how blessed you are or how deprived you feel? Are you letting those prickly pears needle you when you can't pay the bills, or can't get something you want, or you get something terrible you don't want? Instead try Mama's way, our Lord's way. It may sound simplistic or a little strange at first, but it works. Start counting your blessings, name each and every one of them. And if you want to go all the way, try humming Mama's favorite chorus.

### FROM GOD'S WORD

O my soul, bless God. / From head to toe, I'll bless his holy name! / O my soul, bless God, / don't forget a single blessing!

(Psalm 103:1-2 MSG)

Whatever is good and perfect is a gift coming down to us from God our Father, who created all the lights in the heavens. He never changes or casts a shifting shadow.

(James 1:17 NLT)

Taste and see that the Lord is good. / Oh, the joys of those who take refuge in him!

(Psalm 34:8 NLT)

### YOUR PRAYER

Dear Father, thank You for Your unfailing love, Your never-ending patience, and Your gracious forgiveness. I am sorry for focusing too often on my burdens and not on Your blessings. Spirit of the Lord, thank You for living in me. From my inside out, grant me the strength to deal with my burdens Your blessed way and not my old way. AMEN.

## 9. ARE YOU ONE OF HIS SHEEP?

WHAT A GIFT WE HAVE in living in the picturesque, rugged, and peaceful Texas Hill Country, but occasionally we must leave our serene hideaway to go to the city. One thing that makes the trip especially enjoyable is driving the country road to the highway and getting to see a flock of sheep tranquilly grazing in the field next to the narrow, winding road.

Recently as we passed by the flock huddled together, I began to think about how Jesus often referred to His followers as His sheep. One day, He recognized that His frightened and confused disciples needed a good dose of encouragement. He used words and imagery that would speak to their hearts. So, He called them His sheep and told them, "I am the good shepherd. The good shepherd sacrifices his life for the sheep" (John 10:11 NLT).

Those famous words of our Lord were for all of His sheep for all times, including sheep like you and me. We're not always good sheep. We don't always follow Him as we should. Sometimes, we wander away and get caught in the brambles just like a feeble lamb. Do you know that if a sheep gets caught in the brambles, he simply lies down, does not eat, and starves to death. Caught in the brambles of life away from our Good Shepherd, our souls are not nourished and we spiritually starve.

And sometimes, like sheep, we're plagued by predators. Let's face it, sheep have it rough. Sheep are known to be weak, slow, vulnerable, and easily led astray. And there always seems to be a stronger, faster, cleverer, and downright crueler critter out to hurt them. We are prey too. Just like sheep, we slip, fall, get sick, get lost, and fall prey to all kinds of dangers. We need our Shepherd.

Speaking from one needy sheep to another, the good news from Jesus is clear: No matter how weak and vulnerable we are, we have the strongest, smartest, most compassionate Good Shepherd in the land, and He has promised to stay with us through it all, even when the wolves would devour us.

There's an ancient Israeli story, or maybe it's a legend. It doesn't matter. In either case, it reminds us of a timeless truth worth remembering.

In long ago time in the rolling hills not far from Jerusalem, there lived a shepherd named Nathaniel. Nathaniel was devoted to caring for his sheep, gathering them, and leading them to a safe place at the end of the day. Before nightfall, he built a roaring campfire to keep the predators away in the dark of night. He was willing to give his life to protect his sheep.

The villagers were impressed with Nathaniel's care for his sheep and the fact that he never lost one sheep, not one. Word of his selfless care for his sheep spread far and wide, reaching even the ears of the king of the land. The king was so inspired by Nathaniel's courage that he invited Nathaniel to his palace and offered him a seat of honor at his table, fine clothes, the offer of work, and the official title as The Greatest Shepherd of the Land.

Nathaniel's response surprised the king and all the villagers, but it did not surprise his sheep. He thanked the king for his gracious offers and explained that he preferred returning to his sheep, to love them, to protect them, and to abide with them. And so, for generations the legend of Nathaniel has brought encouragement to all the *sheep* of the kingdom.

This heartwarming legend reminds all sheep like you and me of a hopeful and encouraging truth. We have an all-loving, all-powerful, all-knowing, and always present Good Shepherd who longs to be with us.

The story of our Good Shepherd is no legend. It's a true story. It's a personal story that includes you and me. You already know it. It's been called the greatest story ever told. It's the story of Jesus, who gave up heaven to come to earth to rescue us. He gave His life so that we could belong to Him.

I am glad I am one of Jesus's sheep. Are you? Like all of us, I know what it's like to be attacked by the wolves of disease, loss, and more. But I also *know* what Jesus said to us sheep in such times. And by *know*, I mean, I have experienced His comforting presence.

Do you see yourself as one of the Good Shepherd's sheep?

## FROM GOD'S WORD

I am the Good Shepherd. The Good Shepherd puts the sheep before himself, sacrifices himself if necessary. A hired man is not a real shepherd. The sheep mean nothing to him. He sees a wolf come and runs for it, leaving the sheep to be ravaged and scattered by the wolf. He's only in it for the money. The sheep don't matter to him. I am the Good Shepherd. I know my own sheep and my own sheep know me. In the same way, the Father knows me and I know the Father. I put the sheep before myself, sacrificing myself if necessary.

(John 10:11-15 MSG)

When he saw the crowds, he had compassion on them because they were confused and helpless, like sheep without a shepherd.

(Matthew 9:36 NLT)

Once you were like sheep who wandered away. But now you have turned to your Shepherd, the Guardian of your souls.

(1 Peter 2:25 NLT)

### YOUR PRAYER

Father, thank You for sending Your son, Jesus, to be my Good Shepherd. As You know, I have been through some difficult days lately. But having You with me all the time and being able to talk to You any time, is a great and comforting gift. And I don't take it for granted, Father. When I look around me, my cup runs over with gratitude as I realize how blessed I am. AMEN.

## 10. ARE YOU A GHOST FLOWER CHRISTIAN?

YOU'D NEVER KNOW THE RARE, perennial ghost flower plant even existed unless you were intentionally looking for it. After all, its flamboyant bloom pops up for only a day between June and September. The two-inch, waxy-white, orchid-like beauty shows off its stunning bloom only briefly when it rises out of its loamy, underground home.

This non-photosynthetic plant has little life above ground. It survives just below the decomposed matter in the darkest parts of the forest floor. Its eerie, iridescent, appearance earned it the mysterious name, *ghost flower*. Being a non-photosynthetic plant means it has no chlorophyll, the chemical that makes the plant green. Without chlorophyll, the plant cannot convert light into energy for food. To survive, it has to steal its nutrients from other plants or fungi beneath the soil.

At first glance, the *Monotropa uniflora* looks like any other friendly, tiny flower in the forest. Let me assure you that it's not. Like most flowers, it has an outward lovely appearance, but it is a self-serving parasite lurking in the darkest parts of the forest looking for food sources.

The more I learned about the ghost flower, the more I noticed some powerful spiritual lessons. As you know, our Lord often taught His disciples important eternal truths by using everyday metaphors like lilies, birds, and other parts of God's creation. Even our creator God used the same kind of metaphors when He taught Job important lessons.

> "Ask the animals, and they will teach you, /
> or the birds in the sky, and they will tell you; /
> or speak to the earth, and it will teach you, /
> or let the fish in the sea inform you. /
> Which of all these does not know /
> that the hand of the Lord has done this? /
> In his hand is the life of every creature /
> and the breath of all mankind."
> (Job 12:7-10 NIV)

So, what lessons might we learn from the ghost flower? Could it be that the ghost flower reminds those of us who claim to be God's children to live in the warmth and energy of His sunlight instead of lurking in the darkness, feeding off the decay of this world? Or perhaps it reminds us that we shouldn't be trying to impress others with a showy, flash-in-the-pan, look-at-me kind of faith while slowly withering away spiritually. We're to be concerned with more than appearances, and we are intended to have a *perennial* faith, not an *annual* one that only lasts for a short season and then is gone. We are intended to be branches that are grafted into Him, the Vine, so that we can grow and produce fruit.

What about you? Are you becoming a ghost flower Christian? I pray not. Occasionally, we all need to stop and take stock of our lives, inside and out. Maybe it's time for you to take a close look and reevaluate your priorities and purposes before you get too far away from Him. Do you believe your Savior is reaching out to you right now, and wants you to come home to Him, to be more committed to nurturing your personal relationship with Him? Is He wanting you to spend more time in the sunlight of His presence, to get closer to His family, to seek His guidance more, and to listen more to His Spirit speaking to you through His Word?

Of course, you don't have to be a ghost flower Christian. You can become what I call a Cedar of Lebanon Christian. The cedar is majestic and mighty and nothing like a showy and short-lived ghost flower. Taking as many as ninety years to grow to its full height, this mighty tree extends its magnificent branches to soak in its Creator's empowering sunlight and buries its hungry roots deep into God's nutritious soil. Stretching into the sky and yet firmly and deeply rooted, the cedar can withstand the wind and the storms. In biblical times, the Cedar of Lebanon was recognized as the tallest, strongest, and most valued tree in that part of the world. Because of its seasoned and beautiful wood grain, kings and emperors sought it to build their temples and palaces.

Today we live in a fast-food, next-day delivery, one-click-away culture. But no matter how much we wish for our relationship with our Lord to be that way, it won't happen. We can pray sincerely and want it with all our hearts. We can even ask the Lord to come into our lives and feel wonderful for a short time. But to be more than a ghost flower Christian and to have a strong, secure, growing, and loving relationship with our Lord, we'll need to take the Cedar of Lebanon way. When we do, we will be able to withstand the harshest of life's storms, and enjoy becoming more like Him, living in His kind of love, joy, and peace. As the scripture says, "And the Lord—who is the Spirit—makes us (gradually) more and more like him as we are changed into his glorious image" (2 Corinthians 3:18 NLT).

The question for today is this, when our Father sees you, does He see a ghost flower Christian or a Cedar of Lebanon Christian?

**FROM GOD'S WORD**

You are like mighty Assyria, which was once like a cedar of Lebanon, with beautiful branches that cast deep forest shade and with its top high among the clouds.

(Ezekiel 31:3 NLT)

What sorrow awaits you teachers of religious law and you Pharisees. Hypocrites! For you are like whitewashed tombs—beautiful on the outside but filled on the inside with dead people's bones and all sorts of impurity.

(Matthew 23:27 NLT)

You must grow in the grace and knowledge of our Lord and Savior Jesus Christ. All glory to him, both now and forever! Amen.

(2 Peter 3:18 NLT)

## YOUR PRAYER

Dear Father, I am ashamed that too often I've thought and acted too much like a ghost glower. And I am deeply sorry. I don't want a faith that is showy and short-lived. I want a faith that is deep and real. Help me, Lord, be more faithful in deepening my spiritual roots. I want to please You and grow in our love. Help me practice daily those things that will help me grow to be one with You. AMEN.

## 11. HAWKS ARE SCARY... OR NOT?

PHYLLIS CALLS OUR AFTERNOON, pre-sunset walks in our Hill Country neighborhood our *little adventures*. They're adventures because we never know what surprises we might encounter. Some days, our surprise is a bird we've never seen before. Other days it's a slithering water moccasin chasing frogs in the swampy pond around the bend.

But one element of our little adventures is not surprising at all. It's quite predictable. While we vary our walks, we first must walk around the pond to get started and to choose our path. On the pond's edge stands a tall, lifeless, leafless tree, its trunk smoothed with age. We wonder sometimes how it could still be standing. Those naked limbs provide the perfect vantage point for a huge hawk that is usually perched on the highest limb, surveilling the pond surface for its evening meal. We get close enough to him to take photos, but not too close.

Perched stealthily above the water, that hawk appears fierce and frightening. His stillness and his penetrating stare keep me cautious. I've seen that hawk drop from his perch like a flash. In a matter of seconds, he has swooped down, captured his prey, and flown back to his favorite limb with a snake in his talons. I've watched the reptile writhe as the hawk pins him to the limb to devour him.

Because of the hawk's appearance and screeching sound, I have assumed they were mean-spirited, aggressive, and dangerous. But after some study, I learned that my assumption was somewhat slanted and incomplete. According to the experts, hawks are highly intelligent, extremely loyal, and unusually nurturing to their young. They can see five times better than humans and use their amazing eyesight to escape threats, stay safe, and hunt for the food God created for hawks. They're basically survivors whose outward appearances are misleading.

That eye-opening truth about the hawk's appearance has been a good reminder for me of the danger of putting too much stock in first impressions. I have a slight tendency to judge a book by its cover. I would probably have taken one look at the empty tomb and quickly concluded someone has stolen Jesus's body. Unfortunately, the inclination to make decisions or judgments based on outward appearances is not new, and neither are our wrong and even hurtful conclusions based on our assumptions.

Probably the most famous Bible story illustrating this problem and God's solution is the story of David's call to be Israel's king. God sent the prophet Samuel to choose one of Jesse's sons as the new king of Israel. Everyone thought Samuel would choose the strongest and tallest brother.

But God's Spirit told Samuel to not choose the most obvious son. "But the Lord said to Samuel, 'Don't judge by his appearance or height, for I have rejected him. The Lord doesn't see things the way you see them. People judge by outward appearance, but the Lord looks at the heart'" (1 Samuel 16:7 NTL).

God not only wanted Samuel to evaluate people and possibilities the way He does, He wants us to do the same. He doesn't want us to value people by the clothes they wear, the kind of cars they drive, the jobs they have, the neighborhoods they live in, or the size of their bank accounts. He wants us to look at what's on the inside.

God wants us to use our spiritual eyes to look for inner qualities like honesty, humility, faithfulness, love, and an unselfish, teachable spirit. Maybe you'll take a little adventure today. And as you do, maybe you'll be conscious of a hawk in your life and your need to reevaluate your assumptions.

## FROM GOD'S WORD

Look beneath the surface so you can judge correctly.

(John 7:24 NLT)

So, we don't look at the troubles we can see now; rather, we fix our gaze on things that cannot be seen. For the things we see now will soon be gone, but the things we cannot see will last forever.

(2 Corinthians 4:18 NLT)

Don't be concerned about the outward beauty of fancy hairstyles, expensive jewelry, or beautiful clothes. You should clothe yourselves instead with the beauty that comes from within, the unfading beauty of a gentle and quiet spirit, which is so precious to God.

(1 Peter 3:3-4 NLT)

## YOUR PRAYER

Dear Father, I am humbled by the thought that so much of the time I value people and things You have given me in the wrong way. I look at their financial value, their outward appearance, or their worth in the minds of the world. Help me follow Jesus's example. I want to look for and admire what's on the inside of people. Guide my spiritual eyes to look for and cherish people's inner qualities like honesty, humility, faithfulness, love, and an unselfishness. AMEN.

## 12. THE SPARROW TAKES CENTER STAGE

I HAVE QUITE THE VIEW from my comfortable *ole* recliner that hugs me like Granny used to do. I only need to turn my head slightly to the right to see the birdfeeder Phyllis's dad built for us. I merely lift my eyes from my laptop computer to enjoy an array of our feathered friends: bright red cardinals, gorgeous gold finches, chickadees, ruby-throated hummingbirds, red-shouldered hawks, long-tailed flycatchers, ever-ravenous doves, and titmice looking like they wore a tuxedo to dinner.

But one thing I know: We have more sparrows than all the other birds combined. Bird experts claim over a billion sparrows are flying around our planet with 245 different kinds of sparrows worldwide. That makes them the most prolific bird on the planet. Filling up our feeders makes me think all billion of them take turns feasting from our deck.

In Jesus's time, like today, sparrows were so common that poor people bought them for their sacrificial offerings when they couldn't afford anything else. It's no wonder Jesus used the ordinary sparrow, not the beautiful cardinal or powerful eagle, as one of the most memorable illustrations in His greatest sermon.

"What is the price of two sparrows—one copper coin? But not a single sparrow can fall to the ground without your Father knowing it" (Matthew 10:29 NLT). What comforting words those must have been to the multitude of ordinary people who listened to Jesus on that hillside overlooking the Sea of Galilee. Too often we all feel like sparrows—ordinary, insignificant, considered of little worth, and forgotten.

Without a doubt, feelings of being worthless, useless, or insignificant are some of the most widespread and painful problems of our time, causing sufferers to self-medicate or grasp at anything to make themselves feel better about themselves. These feelings and emotions affect not only those who are broken, but those of us who are retired seniors, active young people, abused children, and everyone in between.

In our day, the media lauds the sports champions, the super-stars, the award-winners, the most unusual, or most extraordinary among us. With so much attention on the extraordinary, ordinary sparrow-like people like us, often feel like crying, "Does anybody care about me? Do I count at all?"

I believe that's one of the reasons Jesus put the common sparrow above all those colorful, superstar birds. He gave the sparrow center stage that day to remind all of us who are wounded and ordinary-feeling that no matter how forgotten or unimportant we may feel, God does not feel that way. Jesus reminded us that we can't even stumble and fall without God knowing it.

God promises He will never forget you or forsake you. He always values you. He never stops loving you. Some of us have found that during those times when we have felt the lowest or the loneliest, we have heard His inaudible, still, quiet voice whisper, "Don't be afraid. I'm right here with you. I love you, and I always have my eye on you."

I suppose that's why one of my favorite hymns has always been, *His Eye Is on the Sparrow* by Jessi Colter. Does it remind you, of Jesus's comforting words?

> *Why should I feel discouraged, why should the shadows come?*
> *Why should my heart feel lonely and long for Heaven and home,*
> *When Jesus is my portion, a constant friend is He.*

*His eye is on the sparrow, and I know He watches over me.*

*His eye is on the sparrow, and I know He watches me.*

So, every time you see a sparrow, pause and lift your heart to God and quietly say to him, "Thank you Father for caring for ordinary sparrows like me."

### FROM GOD'S WORD

The members of the council were amazed when they saw the boldness of Peter and John, for they could see that they were ordinary men with no special training in the Scriptures. They also recognized them as men who had been with Jesus.

(Acts 4:13 NLT)

I will never fail you. I will never abandon you.

(Hebrews 13:5 NLT)

And I am convinced that nothing can ever separate us from God's love. Neither death nor life, neither angels nor demons, neither our fears for today nor our worries about tomorrow—not even the powers of hell can separate us from God's love. No power in the sky above or in the earth below—indeed, nothing in all creation will ever be able to separate us from the love of God that is revealed in Christ Jesus our Lord.

(Romans 8:38-39 NTL)

## YOUR PRAYER

Father, thank You for loving us ordinary folks just like You care for the sparrows. How grateful I am that I don't have to be a super-star to get Your attention. You said that I cannot fall without Your knowing it. Having You care for me like that and being able to talk to You any time are great and comforting gifts. And I don't take them for granted, Father. When I look around me, my cup runs over with gratitude as I realize how blessed I am. AMEN.

## 13. THE WORST ADVICE I'VE EVER HEARD

As I look back on my forty years of pastoral counseling, I'm sure I didn't always give the best advice, but I'm also sure my counsel did not fall into the category of Paul Hudson's. The pop-culture, amateur advisor gave what I think could be the worst advice I've ever heard on how to have a successful life. He entitled his blog, "Why You Should Never Depend on Anyone But Yourself."

Hudson's counsel is not only misleading but also downright destructive. It may seem macho and impressively independent, but it's not. In his article, he tries to convince people that no one really cares about you and that you're a fool if you think anyone would help you without some devious motive. Hudson said it bluntly, "We are completely alone in this world and anyone that tells you otherwise is simply lying to you... You yourself are the only person that you can and ought to rely on."

Hudson's approach to success reminded me of a middle-aged fellow I'll call Chuck. Chuck was a highly successful businessman envied by everyone in our town. No one would have thought he would feel the need to come for counseling. But what I found when Chuck came to see me was a heavy heart dressed in a two-thousand-dollar suit, a heart about to explode from years of suppressed anger, depression, and most of all sheer loneliness. His condition was the common consequence of going the "I-never-relied-on-anyone-else" approach to life.

In counseling with Chuck, I found he was indeed a wealthy, happy-looking fellow, but he was also a dangerously lonely, friendless, suicidal man. Think about it, what do you suppose happens to a human designed for relationship if that human never depends on or has a close connection with anyone but himself? Would you give that kind of advice to a struggling young heroin addict, an abused wife, a raped teenage girl, a recently informed terminal cancer patient, or a double amputee injured in Afghanistan? I've spent decades listening to hundreds of sad stories like Chuck's—hurting folks fooled by the lie that the way to a happy and successful life is self-reliance.

In one of His most famous metaphorical stories, Jesus taught His disciples that trying to go it alone in life has about as much chance of succeeding as a branch trying to grow fruit without being connected to its life-giving vine. He summarized the story this way, "For apart from me you can do nothing" (John 15:5 NLT).

Too often we live our daily lives in a way that looks like we don't think we really need God or anybody else. But remember, your Creator-God did not create us humans to live alone. In fact, one of the first things He did after creating the first man, Adam, was to create a helpmate for him. The Creator said it clearly. "It is not good for the man to be alone. I will make a helper suitable for him" (Genesis 2:18 NIV).

The same is true for us. From the beginning, the Lord designed us to depend on Him and each other and to help each other, especially during hard times. If you're not in a crisis right now, you're living in what I call the in-between times. None of us is going to escape tough times. We rarely know why bad things happen, but we do know they will happen. We simply live in a fallen world. We can choose to try to handle those times alone, or we can work at handling them God's way.

Think for a moment how Jesus handled His difficult times. Even as capable as He was, being the very Son of God, Jesus didn't try to handle things by Himself. He worked at staying closely connected to His heavenly Father and surrounding Himself with God's family and friends.

Think about what Jesus said were the most important things you can do in your life. When asked what the greatest of all commandments was, Jesus replied, "'You must love the Lord your God with all your heart, all your soul, and all your mind... A second is equally important: 'Love your neighbor as yourself'" (Matthew 22:37-39 NLT).

To love your neighbor as yourself is another way of telling us to care for those whom God puts in your path. When we get wounded by life, we need others. When we stop focusing on our own miseries and be the presence of God for others, we are helped as we give help to the wounded and weary.

So, how can you live out this counter-cultural way? How can you practically put it into practice when you're bombarded by messages from others and media to depend only on yourself? I say, try a different way.

Try Jesus's way. Stay connected to Him and to others. It's the best way. For centuries, it has worked for Christ-followers. It has worked for me personally, and it's been my advice for hurting people for decades. Begin by doing a few simple but essential things. As Jesus reminds us in John 15, we are to abide in Him, to be at home with Him. That means to stay closely connected to Him through talking to Him in prayer and listening to His Spirit through His Word.

Second, make time to be closely connected to a small body of believers. Make them your best friends. Be what the Bible calls a part of the Body of Christ.

Living the Jesus way will not be easy in our culture, but with God and your fellow believers, you can do this. And it will give you the most successful life in the ways that count most.

So which advice do you think is the best? Hudson's advice that it's all up to you and no one else. Or Jesus' advice: Abide in me. Depend on me. Have faith in me. Love one another.

Will you close your eyes right now and tell your waiting Heavenly Father which way you are going from here on?

**FROM GOD'S WORD**

Encourage one another and build each other up.

(1 Thessalonians 5:11 NIV)

Praise be to the God and Father of our Lord Jesus Christ, the Father of compassion and the God of all comfort, who comforts us in all our troubles, so that we can comfort those in any trouble with the comfort we ourselves receive from God.

(2 Corinthians 1:3-4 NIV)

Two are better than one, / because they have a good return for their labor: / If either of them falls down, / one can help the other up. / But pity anyone who falls / and has no one to help them up.

(Ecclesiastes 4:9-10 NIV)

## YOUR PRAYER

Dear Father, I have too long tried to handle things by myself, and I am sorry. I'm ashamed because I know that's not Your way. I know it is against everything I have learned from reading about Your Son, my Lord Jesus. Just as I have depended on You alone to save me, help me, Lord, depend on Your Spirit to work through my life. Help me stop being so self-centered and live daily in a closer relationship with You and the family of faith whom You have given me. AMEN.

## 14. CAN YOU SAY IT IN ONE LINE?

Do you know the difference a well-crafted, one-line statement can make? Many companies do and pay millions of dollars to get marketing firms to help them write those kinds of slogans and mission statements.

For example, do you recognize America's three most memorable company slogans? I'll list the slogans. See if you can name their companies. Here we go: (1) "Just do it", (2) "Think Different", and (3) "When you care enough to send the very best." The correct answers are Nike, Apple, and Hallmark. How did you do?

Those kinds of classic, unforgettable slogans and their companion one-line mission statements don't just happen. They are the results of serious study and focus groups. Those concentrated words are designed to condense the essence of who the company is and what its main goals are. Such memorable and succinct one-liners have proven to be worth every penny.

Experts have found if organizations cannot write their main goal in one line, they clearly do not yet have a good handle on who they are, why they exist, and what their goals and objectives are. One-liners give them focus and a hitching post.

The same is true for us as Christians. If we can't write in one line what our main goals or values are, often called our mission statements, we don't really know what they are and we're certainly going to miss those things we want most.

Jesus knew the importance of one-liners. He often used them to clarify who He was and what He considered most important. His one-liners were simple, unforgettable, and quotable. They have all made a lasting impression on our lives. Can you recall some of them? Here are a few of my favorites.

- "I am the way, the truth, and the life." (John 14:6 NLT)
- "I have come down from heaven to do the will of God who sent me, not to do my own will. (John 6:38 NLT)
- "My Father! If it is possible, let this cup of suffering be taken away from me. Yet I want your will to be done, not mine." (Matthew 26:39 NLT)

- "I am the good shepherd. The good shepherd sacrifices his life for the sheep." (John 10:11 NLT)

Jesus's one-liners and His descriptions of His main reasons for leaving heaven and coming to us are still today powerful reminders of who He is, what His character is like, and what He cares about most. We look to His carefully chosen words to help us choose our goals and our values.

How can thoughtfully putting into one sentence your most cherished values and primary purposes in life be helpful to you?

1. It will help you stay focused: A mission statement will help you stay lasered in on what matters most to you. It will be your moral and spiritual compass, keeping you on track with your core values and goals.
2. It will help you avoid temptations: A well-crafted mission statement will keep you from getting distracted. You're more likely to reach your most important goals because you're not distracted by things that have lesser purposes. It will keep you from yielding to poor choices, and will help you to make better decisions, ensuring that your choices will work towards God's best for you.

3. It will help inspire you: A well-crafted mission statement will help you by being a constant source of inspiration and motivation so that you don't get weary in doing good. When challenging times come, it will help reignite your passion and commitment to keep you going and striving. It will always remind you of why you started in the first place.

Every time you're faced with making a choice and are not sure what to do, you'll look to your mission statement and ask yourself, "Will what I am about to do help me reach my goals for serving Christ and getting God's best for me or will this choice hurt me and my relationship to God?"

As you can see, having these goals clear and available is critical for making daily decisions. Without them, we are left to our momentary urges. Why not write your mission statement and be ready in advance? It's not as easy as you might think. But if you put your mind and heart to it, your Lord will guide you and you can do it. When you complete it, it will help you in all the ways I have outlined and probably even more ways.

Below is my personal mission statement that I wrote many years ago and still use today. Feel free to use it as an example.

*"What I want most is to have an intimate relationship with my Heavenly Father, to put His will above mine, to love my wife and family like Christ loved me and gave Himself for me, and to care for His children above myself, and to serve God with all my resources no matter the circumstances."*

So, what do you say? Is the Lord telling you to give it a try? You might want to begin your one-line mission statement with these words, "What I want most is…"

### FROM GOD'S WORD

(Jesus said) My purpose is to give them a rich and satisfying life.

(John 10:10 NLT)

Don't copy the behavior and customs of this world, but let God transform you into a new person by changing the way you think. Then you will learn to know God's will for you, which is good and pleasing and perfect.

(Romans 12:2 NLT)

Examine yourselves to see if your faith is genuine. Test yourselves.

(2 Corinthians 13:5 NLT)

## YOUR PRAYER

Dear Father, as I honestly look over my past and how I've made decisions, I am ashamed how often I have not given a thought about what is most important to me. I've not considered those values, and beliefs You gave me when I started following Jesus. I am sorry that I have ignored listening to Your Spirit speak to my mind and heart. Help me Lord to be more disciplined about putting first things first. Guide me to look to Your goals for my every choice and not merely trust my impulses. I sincerely want to please You, Lord. AMEN.

## 15. JAIRUS: TURN YOUR BELIEFS INTO FAITH

THE LITTLE GIRL HAD ALREADY DIED by the time Jesus arrived. The family and crowd, seeing Him, thought, "There is nothing He can do." But was there? Two thousand years later, we all know He could and did perform a miracle.

Jesus gently took her hand and whispered two words in her native tongue, *"Talitha Koumi,"* meaning, "Get up, little girl." Immediately, she arose. Where only moments ago lay a lifeless body, now stood a vibrant twelve-year-old, smiling as she beheld Jesus (Mark 5:21-43 NLT).

For centuries, countless of us have drawn inspiration, hope, and guidance from this gripping story. As we focus our attention on Jairus (pronounced Jy-rus), we find lessons that make a big difference in our daily lives and, for some, in their eternal lives.

Jairus is not the main character in this story, nor is the story's central message about his faith. The main character is Jesus, and the core message is that Jesus, the all-loving, all-powerful Son of God, can do anything—even raise a little girl from the dead. Yet, if you look closely, you'll see a secondary message that feels like the main message to those of us facing life's toughest challenges. It's the comforting reality that Jesus, the very Son of God, never forgets us in our pain and is always ready to whisper, "Get up, my child. I am here for you. I'm here to help you rise from whatever you're going through."

But let's look at Jairus. He was a good, self-made man, a devoted churchman, beloved by all, and a community leader. He was successful and accustomed to handling everything on his own until one day when a personal crisis struck. His daughter fell gravely ill. Fear, frustration, and feelings of helplessness consumed him. He had always known what to do, always found solutions, but not this time. His financial success and dedication to his beliefs offered no help. His sweet daughter was dying, and he was powerless.

But Jairus had heard of Jesus, the miracle worker, who was now in the town of Capernaum. Jairus had heard friends give their testimonies of witnessing Jesus's works firsthand. So, he made a choice. His beliefs were insufficient; he needed help beyond himself. He took a leap of faith, a chance, and sought out Jesus. In an act of genuine faith, Jairus pushed through the crowd, fighting for an audience with Him.

Jairus did something extremely difficult for him and for most of us. He humbly admitted he could not handle things by himself any longer. He opened his heart and mind, asking for help. When Jesus saw Jairus struggling to get to him, Jesus recognized Jairus's determination as genuine faith, not mere belief. He accepted Jairus's trust, answered his plea, and followed Jairus to his home where his daughter lay dead. Jesus honored his faith. That's when the miracle happened.

As time ran out for his little girl, Jairus felt frantic and weak. He felt afraid and confused over unanswered prayers. Like Jairus, we have all felt the sting of uncontrollable grief, anger, and doubt when we are overwhelmed by fear, frustration and helplessness, when our religious beliefs and activities fall short. We must make the plunge Jairus made. In Jairus, I see a reflection of myself when crises have hit me, and perhaps you do too.

Jairus's story teaches us the power of a personal, relentless faith, a faith that is more than ritual and earnest beliefs. We should ask ourselves, "Is my entire religion really no more than a system of beliefs and religious activities?" We'll never find a personal relationship with our Lord just from having correct beliefs. Beliefs don't always make us obedient followers. In fact, in many cases, beliefs can prevent us from being true Christ-followers. Like Jairus and his daughter, when we choose to trust ourselves into His strong, tender hands, we will feel and be safe and at peace even in our darkest moments with pain, sickness, or even death.

Jairus's story has reminded me, and I hope it will remind you, to move beyond the mere motions of religion and develop a loving, personal, trusting relationship with Jesus. Real faith is depending on Jesus with our heads, hearts, bodies, and souls. It's holding on to Him and waiting on Him through any storm. It's trusting Him to be who He says He is in His Word, trusting Him with His timetable to bring life where there is death, hope where there is despair, healing where there is brokenness, and purpose where there seems to be none.

In those days and nights when you struggle with difficult trials, will you join me in re-reading Jairus's story? Will you remember what he did by turning from being a man of mere beliefs to a man who risked taking the step of genuine faith? Aren't we grateful that our hope no longer rests on our own understanding and our own strength but on the loving, faithful, all-knowing, and all-powerful presence of our Lord Jesus?

And here's a final word I have for you. When life gets especially tough, if you listen closely, you just might hear our Lord whisper in the ear of your conscience with His inaudible voice, "Get up, my little child. It's going to be all right!"

**FROM GOD'S WORD**

I have told you all this so that you may have peace in me. Here on earth you will have many trials and sorrows. But take heart, because I have overcome the world.

(John 16:33 NLT)

We are pressed on every side by troubles, but we are not crushed. We are perplexed, but not driven to despair. We are hunted down, but never abandoned by God. We get knocked down, but we are not destroyed.

(2 Corinthians 4:8-9 NLT)

But those who trust in the Lord will find new strength. / They will soar high on wings like eagles. / They will run and not grow weary. / They will walk and not faint.

(Isaiah 40:31 NLT)

## YOUR PRAYER

Dear Father, thank You for Your care and understanding of me in all of my circumstances. I am constantly astonished and grateful for how accessible You are to me when You have so many children in much greater need than I am. But I trust Your Word when You say to come to You anytime. Today, I ask You as humbly as I know how to give me Your inner peace and strength to do as Jairus did, to keep getting up and keep going no matter how difficult it is at times. Lead me to accept and do Your will, Lord. AMEN.

# 16. JAIRUS: TURN YOUR PAIN INTO YOUR PROJECT

PHYLLIS AND I ARE HIGHLY PREDICTABLE PEOPLE, and we like it that way. We say it just makes life easier. Every day starts the same: we get up together, make the bed together, and brush our teeth together. You can imagine the rest of our day. Normally, our days are so routine we could almost do them with our eyes closed. But not this particular day.

This day was anything but routine. Phyllis had just finished dressing and headed to the kitchen. When I turned to follow her, I felt a little dizzy. The room started spinning. I didn't say anything to Phyllis because I didn't want to frighten her. Besides, I figured it was nothing and would probably pass in a minute. But it didn't. The room kept spinning. So, I backed up to the sink, grabbed hold of it trying to steady myself. My legs felt so weak that I began wilting to the floor. Everything went black.

When I woke up, the EMS guy in the back of the ambulance with me said, "You're on the way to the University Hospital. I've called ahead. Don't worry about a thing. They'll take good care of you. You're going to be okay."

When we got to the hospital, there was no available room. So, I was stuck in the ER with a continuous wave of nurses and specialists checking me out. When I got to my room, one of the hospital's neurologists, who examined the scans of my head stepped in. With a poker-face he said, "Dr. Nichols, our tests show that you've had a stroke." His words hit me like a ton-of-bricks. "A stroke? Not me. This can't be happening." I couldn't believe what I just heard.

Phyllis and I were frozen. We held our breath wondering what he would say next. Our faces must have signaled how shocked we were from his news. He quickly said, "But Dr. Nichols, it looks like your stroke is what we consider mild. And more than likely, you'll recover fully over time." What a relief indeed! Unfortunately, the doctor's prognosis was a little off. I am over the worst of it, but I'm still working on that *fully recovered* part. The rehab process has been slow and discouraging at times.

As a former pastor, counselor, and hospital chaplain, too many times before, I've seen people's recovery process change them. Before their crisis, they were happy, positive thinking, other-centered, and grateful-to-God kind of people who turned into negative, angry, bitter, depressed, self-centered, sick people. If we're not careful, even we people of faith can let our crisis control our minds, hearts, and entire lives.

But we don't have to give the crisis control. The choice is ours. We can choose to take control of how we respond to our problems, whether they're physical, financial, relational, emotional, or any other kind of problem. The beginning step to getting control of the situation is to get up from your problem and turn it into a project. Decide it's your new job. Design yourself a plan. Set realistic goals. Take little steps. Work your plan. Stay on schedule. Find a friend who listens to your complaints but will encourage you, keep you moving, help you get up when you're knocked down, and keep you focused on your goal.

Remember that's what Jairus did with his challenging crisis. He had a bit of a stroke himself. An emotional stroke. When his young daughter was dying and there was no doctor, no hospital, no apparent cure for what she had, he was paralyzed. No matter how hard he tried, this time he could not handle things himself. So, he made a choice.

Jairus turned his problem into a project. The project was to get help from someone who could save his daughter. His first step was to get up and find Jesus, whom he had heard was in town and was known for doing miracles. He would get to Jesus no matter the roadblocks. As you remember, he stuck to his plan, and in faith didn't give up until Jesus came back to his house and raised his daughter from the dead.

At times, we're all in Jairus's situation, we simply cannot handle our problem. In those times, we can count on the Spirit of the Lord to tell those of us who are paralyzed from a stroke, or pain, or heartache, "Get up, little child. Don't give up. Keep going. I have things for you to do." Join me and Paul the apostle in saying "We are pressed on every side by troubles, but we are not crushed. We are perplexed, but not driven to despair. We are hunted down, but never abandoned by God. We get knocked down, but we are not destroyed" (2 Corinthians 4:8-9 NLT).

## FROM GOD'S WORD

So, let's not get tired of doing what is good. At just the right time we will reap a harvest of blessing if we don't give up.

(Galatians 6:9 NLT)

The Lord hears his people when they call to him for help. / He rescues them from all their troubles. / The Lord is close to the brokenhearted; / he rescues those whose spirits are crushed.

(Psalm 34:17-18 NLT)

The godly may trip seven times, but they will get up again.

(Proverbs 24:16 NLT)

### YOUR PRAYER

Dear Father, as I honestly look over my past, I see times when I was paralyzed by fear or confusion and I failed to trust You. Help me keep my eyes on You, and help me to focus on turning my pain and confusion into a project, into something that can make a difference to me and someone else. Help me to remember that You are present with me. How grateful I am that You don't hide, but You're always accessible. AMEN.

## 17. HARD WORK IS THE KEY TO SUCCESS. OR IS IT?

FROM MY EARLIEST MEMORY, my dad taught me to live by Booker T. Washington's aphorism, "Nothing ever comes to one, that is worth having, except as a result of hard work." My dad saw to it that Washington's old saying became my eleventh commandment. And for years, Dad's way worked, until it didn't.

It is true that most successful people in any area of life worked hard and sacrificed greatly to get where they are. No one would disagree that hard work is crucial to success. But an even more important fact is this: people who find success in the things that are the most valuable in this world will tell you that behind the scenes the true source of all the good we have honestly comes from God's grace.

Nobody believes that fact more passionately than David Green, the founder of Hobby Lobby. It took him a while to get it but when he did, it made a big difference in his life. David started out poor but was dedicated to hard work. He eventually saved up enough money to launch his first retail store in 1970 with only $600 in start-up capital. Over time, he turned that meager amount into an empire employing over 43,000 people in 900 stores. Now his personal fortune exceeds $14 billion, making him one of the richest people in the world.

As a child, David adopted the same work ethic my dad taught me. David listened faithfully to that same old convincing, inner voice that was nothing more than a half-truth, "If you want to succeed, work hard, sacrifice everything, and put work first."

That popular American lie seemed to work for him for a while. But in time, it produced more than financial success. It produced an anxious spirit and a persistent sense of emptiness. David's life was consumed from dawn till dusk with work to expand his business empire. Despite all his so-called successes, there was an obvious void. Something was missing and that something kept him feeling anxious with a soulful yearning for that something more.

During that dark period of searching, David read a familiar childhood Bible verse he felt was just for him, "God saved you by his grace when you believed. And you can't take credit for this; it is a gift from God. Salvation is not a reward for the good things we have done, so none of us can boast about it" (Ephesians 2:8-9 NLT).

The reading of that particular scripture was a turning point for David. It was a penetrating reminder of a truth he had long overlooked. As successful as he was, David recognized that his outstanding efforts were not the conclusion of it all. He realized that everything he had that was truly good ultimately did not come from his efforts but from God himself.

David once told a gathering of business leaders, "It is by God's grace and provision that Hobby Lobby has endured. Therefore, we seek to honor God by operating the company in a manner consistent with biblical principles."

With his new worldview, David's entire life-perspective shifted dramatically. He began to view his personal and work life not as a series of business milestones to conquer but as a series of steps in his journey of gratitude and service to his gracious Lord. He once put it this way, "True wealth is about more than money. If you have anything, or if I have anything, it's because it's been given to us by our Creator."

One example of David's transformational change was the new way he looked at his business. The media and his business associates were shocked when David made his unthinkable business decision to close all of his Hobby Lobby stores on Sundays to give employees time to worship and be with family. A decision that seemed foolish to the retail world, it was predicted to cause a massive financial loss. However, David approached his decision with a deep sense of inner peace. He felt he was doing the right thing for his employees and demonstrating faith in God. He prayed for guidance, trusted in God's leadership, and moved forward without the crippling pressure of his old belief system—the system claiming that everything depended on his own smarts and hard work.

The outcome was remarkable. Not only did Hobby Lobby continue to thrive financially, but his decision also brought him a profound sense of being in God's will. David's understanding of success was irrevocably transformed. He discovered that true success was not measured by the amount of his financial gain or business accolades but by the depth of his relationship with his Lord and the joy of living and serving others. His life, once motivated by a persistent pursuit of achievement became driven by an overpowering desire to express his gratitude for God's generosity.

Today, David Green is an inspiration to millions. I pray that his story will be an encouragement to you as it has been for me. I hope it will remind you of the powerful but often-forgotten truth in our work-obsessed society—while hard work and dedication are important ingredients of worldly success, true success and joy in all the most important parts of our lives ultimately come from a close relationship with our Lord and from demonstrating our gratitude to Him.

By the way, it's easy to correct Booker T. Washington's half-truth aphorism and make it true. Simply add two important words, "Nothing ever comes to one, that is worth having, except as a result of *God's grace* and hard work."

### FROM GOD'S WORD

He saved us, not because of the righteous things we had done, but because of his mercy. He washed away our sins, giving us a new birth and new life through the Holy Spirit.

(Titus 3:5 NLT)

For by grace you have been saved through faith. And this is not your own doing; it is the gift of

God, not a result of works, so that no one may boast.

(Ephesians 2:8-9 NIV)

We know very well that we are not set right with God by rule-keeping but only through personal faith in Jesus Christ. How do we know? We tried it—and we had the best system of rules the world has ever seen! Convinced that no human being can please God by self-improvement, we believed in Jesus as the Messiah so that we might be set right before God by trusting in the Messiah, not by trying to be good.

(Galatians 2:16 MSG)

## YOUR PRAYER

Dear Father, I am ashamed to confess that at times I have considered my hard work and self-achievement as how I've gotten everything I have. I'm so sorry, Lord. I know better. Kindly help me stop listening to that old, false, deceptive inner voice and listen to Your Spirit speak the truth to my mind and heart. I realize that all I have ultimately comes from You. Receive my gratitude for Your forgiveness, patience, and overwhelming grace. AMEN.

## 18. STAY CONNECTED

FOR YEARS, TOGETHER PHYLLIS AND I led mission groups to Guatemala. One year she led the team without me while I was recovering from an illness. My doctors insisted that I should not make the trip. So, off she went on her own.

I was proud to be married to the kind of woman who would sacrificially organize, train, and lead a group of medical students, doctors, and other volunteers to a region of the world that our State Department classified as unsafe. She and her team were unselfishly brave to provide physical and spiritual care for a small group of girls in an isolated, village orphanage in the Highlands of Guatemala.

From the moment they left, I prayed for them. But honestly, I prayed mostly for Phyllis. We'd always gone together before, and when together, I knew if she was safe or not. We've always been one of those inseparable couples that do everything together. And even if we are separated for a short time, we stay in touch.

This time she was in a mountainous jungle region, and telecommunications were sparse. We were completely cut off from communicating with each other. And I felt lonely, fearful, and just plain miserable. I desperately wanted to hear her voice. I wanted to know she was safe and not sick or in danger.

I breathed a deep sigh of relief when she finally got to a nearby town and I heard her sweet voice, "Hello, Love. We're all doing fine." Isn't it amazing how, for human relationships, a simple word that reconnects us to someone we love brings so much comfort? The same is true for our spiritual relationship with our loving Lord. Just staying connected brings so much joy, peace, and courage to carry on.

When Jesus was about to return to His heavenly Father, He used a brief, down-to-earth word-picture lesson to prepare His disciples to carry on His mission while they were temporarily separated. Through masterful metaphor, He reminded them of the secret to His own power on earth—the source of His strength that kept Him going when it seemed like everything was against Him.

He began His famous descriptive instruction with this memory-worthy, summary sentence, "I am the vine, and you are the branches" (John 15:5 NIV). Jesus went on to explain that as a branch I must abide, that is, to stay connected to the vine or I will shrivel up and die.

He made it simple. The choice is clear. Stay connected and flourish. Receive the vine's life-giving nutrients and no matter your circumstances, you will thrive and bear much fruit. Or you can exercise your willfulness and try going it alone, letting things pull you away, and you will become disconnected and wither away. Disconnected, you will spiritually dry up and will bear no fruit.

Even the very Son of God repeatedly confessed He could do absolutely nothing on His own. (John 5:30) He needed to stay connected. The same is true for you. You need to see yourself as His branch, reminding yourself that you are grafted into Him, your life-giving, nourishing vine. You can't make it unless you keep receiving His spiritual power and love. Your main job is to stay connected to Him, never allowing anything to disconnect you from Him.

Life has always been hard for God's children, but those who have stayed connected to Him have overcome their hardships.

Take Joseph. The favored son. The most-likely-to-succeed. Then a victim of his jealous brothers. He was trafficked into slavery and unjustly imprisoned with no apparent way out. But God had a plan, and Joseph was obedient. His life turned around. Freed from prison, he eventually rose to be the second most powerful man in Egypt. How did he survive and thrive? He stayed connected to the vine.

Take Moses. The heir to the throne. Everything was going well for him in the house of the Pharaoh. Then he lost it all and was hopelessly exiled to the desert. But, like with Joseph, God had a plan. Moses was obedient, and his life completely turned around. He returned to Egypt, rescued his people, crossed the Red Sea on dry ground, and reached the Promised Land. How did he survive and thrive? He stayed connected to the vine.

The same could be said of young David who faced the giant Goliath, or Queen Esther, who faced the annihilation of her people, or many other men and women in Biblical history who faced life's painful challenges. This list is long. But the answer to how they were able to survive and thrive is short. They were branches who stayed connected to the vine.

Life is often complicated for all of us. If we are not deliberate and careful, those prickly-pear situations and even our pride-filled successes will come between us and our Lord. It's easy to get disconnected, discouraged, and disheartened.

So, today, in all of your busyness, in all of Satan's temptations, in all of your heartaches, and even in all of the good things you are doing, don't forget the main thing.

I don't need to tell you what it is. You know what it is. And you can say it in only two words. Fill in the blank.

_____  _____.

## FROM GOD'S WORD

Come close to God, and God will come close to you. Wash your hands, you sinners; purify your hearts, for your loyalty is divided between God and the world.

(James 4:8 NLT)

The Lord is close to all who call on him, / yes, to all who call on him in truth.

(Psalm 145:18 NLT)

Then Jesus said, "Come to me, all of you who are weary and carry heavy burdens, and I will give you rest."

(Matthew 11:28 NLT)

## YOUR PRAYER

Dear Father, I am amazed and humbled just to know that You love me and want to be close to me. Although I don't always show it enough, I love You with all my heart, and I want to stay closely connected to You. Help me do whatever I need to do to make that the main thing I do. AMEN.

## 19. OH! TO FLY FREE AS A BIRD!

JUST BEFORE THE SUN DROPPED behind the small mountain that shades our home, Phyllis grabbed her binoculars and I strapped on my camera. We headed to a patch of oak trees near a pond where a family of Vermillion flycatchers lives.

We found our favorite spot and sat quietly waiting. Because Phyllis has eagle eyes, she's the one in charge of spotting those three-inch, scarlet birds, and I sit, poised with my camera waiting for her to point. Within minutes, she silently directed my attention to a bird leaving its perch. I aimed my camera, and I got several of those rare, split-second shots of that winged ball-of-fire as he darted to catch the wind currents.

Oh, to be free to glide and soar! I've always wished I could fly. Just to be free as a bird. Have you ever longed for that kind of freedom?

We humans have been wishing and trying to soar like birds for thousands of years. King David wanted to fly. Nearly three thousand years ago, he was so tired of his enemies and personal problems

David wrote, "Oh, that I had wings like a dove; then I would fly away and rest!" (Psalm 55:6 NLT).

At the core of how God made us is this relentless desire to be free. To escape all that tethers us and holds us back. To just let go and sail away into our dreams and visions. Maybe that restless, heartfelt longing deep within us for freedom, inner peace, and contentment is the source of the old idiom: "I want to be free as a bird."

The Bible is a series of true stories about our Creator-Savior God, who, since creation has been doing all He can to set His children free. He wants us to be free from the all the things that bind us: our fears, misplaced priorities, consequences of our bad choices, unhealthy relationships, and prideful behavior. He wants us to be free to be all He designed us to be.

The best true story in all the Bible is about our Heavenly Father sending His son to the world to *save* us. I love that power-packed, picture-word *save*. It literally means to *set free*. Imagine a bird with its wings trussed to its body. It's alive. It is designed to fly. It wants to fly. But it can't do or be what God designed it to do and be because its wings are restrained. With all its strength, the bird has tried many times to free itself, but it just can't do it. It needs someone who cares to cut it loose. To *set it free*. It needs a savior.

We all go through times when we feel like that little bird, bound and constrained. Possibly for some time, you've been going through some difficulty. Maybe the difficulty is the consequence of bad choices you've made or someone else made. Maybe you don't even know what caused it. What you do know for certain is that you feel like that modest, tied-up bird. Part of the time you feel frustrated and ready to give up. Other times you feel angry and alone. Most of the time you just want what David wanted: to sprout wings and fly away from all your problems to some quiet, restful place where you are free and able to experience all God desires for you.

I've been there myself. I know how it feels to be like that helpless little bird. But I was set free. Years ago, in faith, I asked Jesus to do for me what I could not do for myself. He answered my simple prayer and immediately started setting me free and has ever since. Day by day, sometimes minute by minute, He's kept on freeing me by forgiving me, guiding me, calming me, empowering me, and freeing me through His indwelling presence.

So, let me assure you, being free is much more and much better than I ever imagined. I hope you'll begin today experiencing that joyful freedom. Maybe your time to be set free is right now. Ask the Spirit of Jesus to come into your life and start setting every part of you free each day and for eternity so you can soar to new heights and be free as a bird.

## FROM GOD'S WORD

The Scriptures declare that we are all prisoners of sin, so we receive God's promise of freedom only by believing in Jesus Christ.

(Galatians 3:22 NLT)

Christ has set us free to live a free life. So take your stand! Never again let anyone put a harness of slavery on you.

(Galatians 5:1 MSG)

For it is by believing in your heart that you are made right with God, and it is by openly declaring your faith that you are saved.

(Romans 10:10 NLT)

## YOUR PRAYER

Dear Father, I am sorry that I let myself get tied up and bound by the things of this world. I ask for Your forgiveness. My deepest desire is to be set free by Your Spirit. I want to be able to live in a way that pleases You and brings us close. Help me surrender my whole self: my head, heart, and hands to Your indwelling Spirit so that I might be, spiritually speaking, free as a bird. AMEN.

## 20. DELIGHT IN YOUR DIFFICULTIES

THE TITLE "DELIGHT IN YOUR DIFFICULTIES," may sound like a gimmick. It's not, but it surely poses an intriguing question. Can we truly find delight in our worst struggles? We all face challenges, whether it be a chronic illness, broken relationship, or emotional pain. We all wish we could embrace them instead of fighting them.

The good news is that there are rare instances where a book or article actually delivers as much as it promises and genuinely transforms lives. What if this were such an article that would help you find such a transformation of your difficulty, disability, or dilemma, bringing you joy and a sense of value and purpose?

The Apostle Paul experienced this firsthand. For years, he endured a persistent ailment, referred to as his "thorn in the flesh." He pleaded with God to remove it. Instead, God revealed a different way. He helped Paul find more than he asked for. He helped him find delight in his difficulty.

Here's how Paul put it. "To keep me from becoming conceited, I was given a thorn in my flesh... Three times I pleaded with the Lord to take it away from me. But he said to me, 'My grace is sufficient for you, for my power is made perfect in weakness.' Therefore, I will boast all the more gladly about my weaknesses, so that Christ's power may rest on me. That is why, for Christ's sake, I delight in weaknesses, in insults, in hardships, in persecutions, in difficulties. For when I am weak, then I am strong" (2 Corinthians 12:7-10 NIV).

Paul once viewed his thorn as a burden to bear, but the Lord helped him with his perspective to see it as a gift to use. Not a pleasant gift. But a painful gift like Jesus's cross was to Him: an excruciating job Jesus did for the good of others to carry out His Father's purpose for Him.

I feel a bit like Paul. For a long time, I too have had a thorn in my flesh that has never completely gone away, but our Lord showed me what He showed Paul.

From a young age, I always felt like I didn't quite fit in. School was challenging for me. Every assignment and all tests were just too difficult for me. I especially struggled with reading out loud, and that made me an easy target for ridicule from my classmates. Eventually, my teacher moved me to the remedial class. The kids cruelly referred to it as the *stupid-kids-class*. I guarantee you, it hurt deeply. I felt different and stupid.

My loving parents assured me I was not stupid at all. They explained that I just had different interests and talents, such as art, music, and doing creative projects. They told me God had a unique purpose for me that He would reveal to me at just the right time. Unbeknownst to me at that time, I was born with relatively common brain-based learning disorder called dyslexia. Affecting about ten percent of the population, dyslexia is a learning disability that makes it more difficult to process language, especially written language.

Inspired by God's Word and the testimonies of many others with severe difficulties, I began to see my *thorn in the flesh* as an opportunity for growth, perseverance, and motivation to carry out the Lord's purposes for me. I could share with you many stories of others who have experienced the Lord's transforming way of viewing their *thorn in the flesh*, but I will share just a few.

Most people are not aware that the national award-winning author, John Irving faced severe challenges due to his dyslexia. Like me as a boy, he suffered the humiliation and the difficulties with reading and writing. He remembers that everyone treated him as lazy and stupid because they were unaware of his condition.

However, Irving's passion for writing persisted. He was determined to prove them wrong. He turned his difficulty into a relentless determination. He now believes that if any of us want to overcome a disadvantage we must work harder, repeat any simple task over and over, and pay extra attention to details. We must make a firm decision in advance to use our particular problem as a source of strength rather than weakness. And just look what happened to John Irving. He won national acclaim for his writing.

When I worked in television, we had a beautiful, talented, upbeat, independent, Christian actress who hosted her own children's TV series sponsored by Mattel Toys. She did mind-boggling things to entertain and inspire her audience.

On her show, she once let a tarantula crawl in her hand and a tiger clamp its jaws around her arm. She danced, parachuted out of a plane, rode an elephant, went snow-skiing, and scuba-diving. She even went bungee jumping.

Oh, yes. Did I mention Kim is also deaf and blind? Once when Kim and I approached an advertising executive about being a sponsor for her show, he asked if she ever thought the medical field would one day find a way for her to see again. She surprised him with her answer, "I don't really have time to worry about that. I'm too busy enjoying doing my show."

What I heard Kim saying is what she had said many times before as a disability rights advocate. "I would never be where I am today if it were not for who I am. I'm grateful that my disability has given me the chance to use my abilities in ways I never thought possible."

We all have difficulties. Some are more severe and more obvious than others. Whatever your difficulty, I pray you will start thinking about it in a new way, the way that changed the Apostle Paul and so many others. Try looking at it through the eyes of faith.

Your difficulty, weakness, or limitation will appear different, a good kind of different. You'll no longer see your difficulty as a disadvantage, but an advantage. You'll be more grateful to your Lord than you have ever been. Paul put it this way, "I will boast all the more gladly about my weaknesses, so that Christ's power may rest on me. That is why, for Christ's sake, I delight in weaknesses, in insults, in hardships, in persecutions, in difficulties. For when I am weak, then I am strong" (2 Corinthians 12:8-10 NIV).

Are you ready to say with Paul and the rest of us, "I have gratefully discovered the Lord's way. I now delight in my difficulties?"

## FROM GOD'S WORD

Dear brothers and sisters, when troubles of any kind come your way, consider it an opportunity for great joy. For you know that when your faith is tested, your endurance has a chance to grow. So let it grow, for when your endurance is fully developed, you will be perfect and complete, needing nothing.

(James 1:2-4 NLT)

Be thankful in all circumstances, for this is God's will for you who belong to Christ Jesus.

(1 Thessalonians 5:18 NLT)

We do not lose heart. Though our outer self is wasting away, our inner self is being renewed day by day. For this light momentary affliction is preparing for us an eternal weight of glory beyond all comparison, as we look not to the things that are seen but to the things that are unseen. For the things that are seen are transient, but the things that are unseen are eternal.

(2 Corinthians 4:16-18 NLT)

## YOUR PRAYER

Father, I come to You with a most grateful heart. You know how I've looked at my *thorn in the flesh*. It has been difficult at times. At times I have felt like Paul, praying You would take it away. Help me, Lord, be able to delight in my difficulties. Help me to use anything and everything that comes my way as an opportunity to serve You. AMEN.

## 21. HE'S WATCHING YOU

MY PLANE WAS LATE, and I had a two-hour drive ahead of me. If I wanted to hear Phyllis sing way out in the Hill Country at the spiritual retreat, I would have to speed a little. But I figured I had a good excuse. Guess what? The highway patrolman whose radar caught me wasn't influenced by what I thought was a heartwarming excuse. To him, I had broken the law, and I had to pay a hefty fine.

Some folks see God as a sort of patrolman-in-the-sky with His supernatural radar, watching and waiting to catch us. If that is how you view God, then your perception is distorted. He's not watching and hoping that He'll catch you messing up. He watches over you to catch you from falling into big trouble.

How you picture the Lord's watchful presence makes an enormous difference in how you handle your difficult days. The Bible's primary depiction of the Lord is not that of a heartless God peeking over your shoulder with a notepad in hand jotting down your every sin. Not at all.

God's Word portrays God as a loving, caring, ever-present Father who brought you into this world because He wanted to love you. And He's faithfully kept His eye on you ever since. He's been watching out for you, looking ahead of you, guiding you, and even holding your hand as He's walked by your side through your darkest of valleys.

I don't know what you or your loved ones are dealing with these days. It may be a painful experience, a relational struggle, serious illness or even death itself, but God's watchful eye knows what's going on in your life. He cares about you, weeps with you, and will be with you no matter what.

Many reporters have written about how a small group of terrorists boarded Flight 93 with the intent of crashing it into the Pentagon on that fateful 9/11 day. They told how the heroic passenger, Todd Beamer, led his fellow passengers to risk their lives to attack the terrorists, keeping that Boeing 757 from crashing into the Pentagon. All forty-four souls on board were killed, but their heroic action prevented the plane from crashing into the Pentagon and taking even more lives. But you may not know what Todd did just before the crash. For me, it was one of the most moving things I've ever read.

In his last moments before he led his fellow passengers to subdue the terrorists and attack the man carrying the bomb, Todd tried to reach his wife by phone, but he was unable. Instead, he reached a telephone operator named Lisa, informing her what was happening and what he was about to do. He also asked her that if he didn't make it to please contact his wife and two sons and tell them how much he loved them. He then requested the operator to pray the Lord's Prayer with him. After that, the chaos began.

The operator could hear as Todd was instructing fellow passengers. Fortunately, the plane's auto voice recorder captured the sounds of the remarkable event. Even with all the screams and other chaotic noises in the background, Todd's voice could be heard reciting the 23rd Psalm as other passengers joined him.

Minutes before their deaths, the chorus of passengers quoted the Shepherd's Psalm, its verses repeatedly echoing the message of God's loving presence and faithful hope even in the face of their darkness and death. Can you imagine what it must have sounded like, hearing all those tearful voices reciting in unison?

"The Lord is my shepherd; I shall not want.

He maketh me to lie down in green pastures: he leadeth me beside the still waters.

He restoreth my soul: he leadeth me in the paths of righteousness for his name's sake.

Yea, though I walk through the valley of the shadow of death, I will fear no evil: for thou art with me; thy rod and thy staff they comfort me.

Thou preparest a table before me in the presence of mine enemies: thou anointest my head with oil; my cup runneth over.

Surely goodness and mercy shall follow me all the days of my life: and I will dwell in the house of the Lord forever" (Psalm 23:1-6 KJV).

At the close of reciting the Psalm, Todd's voice could be heard saying, "Jesus, help me." Then he spoke his famous last words as led his fellow passengers on their mission: "Let's roll."

In this season of your life, you or your loved ones may be facing difficulties you never expected. This snapshot of how Todd Beamer handled the most difficult time in his life gives us a real-life example of how important it is to see God as He really is—the kind of Lord who watches over you all the time. And as the scriptures remind us, He "who watches over you will not slumber. Indeed, he who watches over Israel never slumbers or sleeps. The Lord himself watches over you!" (Psalm 121:3-5).

I pray you will see our Lord as your Shepherd and that you know He is watching over you wherever you are, even when you're walking through the valley of the shadow of death. I pray that His scripture is written in your heart as it was in Todd Beamer's and that it provides comfort and direction for your life every day.

## FROM GOD'S WORD

And I am convinced that nothing can ever separate us from God's love. Neither death nor life, neither angels nor demons, neither our fears for today nor our worries about tomorrow—not even the powers of hell can separate us from God's love. No power in the sky above or in the earth below—indeed, nothing in all creation will ever be able to separate us from the love of God that is revealed in Christ Jesus our Lord.

(Romans 8:38-39 NLT)

Don't be afraid, for I am with you. / Don't be discouraged, for I am your God. / I will strengthen you and help you. / I will hold you up with my victorious right hand.

(Isaiah 41:10 NLT)

Even when I walk through the darkest valley, I will not be afraid, for you are close beside me. Your rod and your staff protect and comfort me.

(Psalm 23:4 NLT)

## YOUR PRAYER

Dear Father, help me focus on Your Holy Word and Your Son's life for my view of You. Help me not to focus on what my culture or customs tell me. Open the eyes of my heart and mind to see Your Spirit's presence in every big and little part of my days and nights. Thank You for always watching over me, not to catch me but to help me. AMEN.

## 22. GOD-BLESSED EYES

A WHILE BACK, I was lying in a hospital bed. The scene was dismal. A gloomy room, gray walls, gray tile floors, tubes, needles, machines, and more beeping machines. We've all experienced those gray, colorless days—days that ambush our focus, preventing us from seeing anything except the bad news, the disappointing results, and unanswered prayers.

Maybe you've been in the doctor's office and you received news that shattered your heart and your hope for the future. Or perhaps you've experienced a painful loss or felt helpless when you couldn't figure a way forward. It's during such heart-wrenching moments when seeing God's presence seems impossible.

I want to tell you about something that happened to me recently while Phyllis and I were taking our usual morning walk in the hills. This particular morning was different, or maybe I was different. Out of nowhere, I felt a cool, refreshing breeze blow across my face and through my hair and was reminded of the wind of His spirit. Shortly after that, I noticed my breathing. Not that anything was wrong. It was just that I was not normally aware of my breathing. Who is?

After our walk that morning, I was sitting out on our deck looking at our lemon tree when I heard the soft buzzing sound of a bumblebee's wings. I turned to locate the little fellow and saw him enjoying the nectar of one of the lemon blossoms. With those and other little attention-grabbers knocking on the door of my mind that morning, I began to wonder what was going on here. Then I began to think about how many of God's attention-grabbers occur all around me on any ordinary day and how many of them I miss—those incredible unnoticed things that would remind me of the Creator who is also my Redeemer, Comforter, and Friend.

No doubt that's the way it is with so many of our Lord's messages. Maybe you're a bit like me. You're so caught up in all that's discouraging, disappointing, or disheartening that you never see much of what He is doing all around you. You miss what He's attempting to show you or say to you. Today, l am challenging you to shift gears. Why not try something new and creative? I promise it will be rewarding.

Starting today, intentionally look and open your heart's eyes to the small and unremarkable-looking ways God is seeking to reveal His loving presence to you. The Apostle Paul said it this way: "No eye has seen, / no ear has heard, / and no mind has imagined / what God has prepared for those who love him" (1 Corinthians 2:9 NLT).

Jesus spoke often about seeing things differently. He once said, "You have God-blessed eyes—eyes that see! And God-blessed ears—ears that hear! A lot of people, prophets and humble believers among them, would have given anything to see what you are seeing to hear what you are hearing, but never had the chance" (Matthew 13:16-17 MSG). Jesus wants us to open our eyes and see things like He does, to look beyond the pain and find God's hand in everything.

It's easy to miss God's Spirit reaching out to us in the little things. We get so caught up in our pain, our worries, and our fears that we too often overlook the whispers of His presence. It could be the warmth of the sun on your face, a kind word from a stranger, or a simple act of love from a friend. The Lord shows up in so many ways, but in our distraction, we don't notice His presence automatically. We have to train our eyes to see Him and our ears to hear Him.

But be careful, seeing God in everything isn't just about finding Him in the good stuff and the beautiful things. It's about recognizing His presence even in our difficult stuff too. His Word reminds us that "God causes everything to work together for the good of those who love God and are called according to his purpose for them" (Romans 8:28 NLT). This doesn't mean everything will be easy or painless. It means that even our toughest times can be part of a bigger plan, one that we might not see or understand right now but can trust is for our ultimate good.

Will you consider taking some holy pauses as you walk the hills of your daily life, to look for God even in all your problems and pain? He will open your eyes to see Him working things out in wonder-making ways you never before imagined possible. It won't be long before you'll find yourself praying something like the words penned by Clara Scott in that favorite old hymn, *Open My Eyes*.

> "Open my eyes that I may see, glimpses of truth Thou hast for me.
> Place in my hands the wonderful key, that shall unclasp and set me free:
> Silently now, I wait for Thee ready, my God, thy will to see;
> Open my eyes, illumine me, Spirit divine."

## FROM GOD'S WORD

Open my eyes so I can see what you show me of your miracle-wonders.

(Psalm 119:18 MSG)

The world cannot receive him (the Holy Spirit), because it isn't looking for him and doesn't recognize him.

(John 14:17 NLT)

So we don't look at the troubles we can see now; rather, we fix our gaze on things that cannot be seen. For the things we see now will soon be gone, but the things we cannot see will last forever.

(2 Corinthians 18:5 NLT)

## YOUR PRAYER

Dear Father, I am sorry that I have missed seeing You moving all around me. I know You're always present, and I know Jesus told His disciples that we do have eyes to see things that only His followers can see. Help me be on the lookout for Your Spirit showing me Your presence in everything You want me to see, always listening for Your Spirit to speak to my mind and heart. I really do want You to open my eyes that I might see all that You want me to see, Lord. AMEN.

## 23. YOU CAN GET ANYTHING IF YOU ASK IN JESUS'S NAME!

THE APOSTLE JOHN HEARD JESUS say it with his own ears, "Yes, ask me for anything in my name, and I will do it" (John 14:14 NLT). His words sound clear, don't they? On the surface, it sounds like Jesus is promising us a blank check—just ask for anything and He's given His word to give it to us. But take another look. Is that really what He was saying?

In my past, I've seen people, including myself at times, caught up in the idea that God is like a cosmic vending machine. Pop in a prayer, out comes our wish. But that's not at all the promise Jesus was communicating.

Take a look at Jesus's own prayer in the garden of Gethsemane. Facing unimaginable agony, He prayed, "Father, if you are willing, please take this cup of suffering away from me. Yet I want your will to be done, not mine" (Luke 22:42 NLT). Notice that Jesus wanted to be relieved of His suffering. In His humanity, He cried out to His Father like we do. We want God to take our miseries from us.

However, look more closely at what Jesus did not say or even imply. He did not say, "Above everything, give me what I want." Not to be misunderstood, Jesus put first things first. He began His prayer by saying, "Father, if you are willing." I agree with some interpreters who translate it like this, "Father, if this is what you want." Whichever translation you choose, they all mean the same thing—above all else, Jesus wanted what His Father wanted.

Here's the point. Under the most unbearable miseries of His life, His words and heart stayed the same. He and His Father had always known such a close relationship that Jesus continually described it this way: "The Father and I are one" (John 10:30 NLT). For Him, they were one in their feelings, thinking, purposes, and desires. He did not attempt to persuade His Father to do what He wanted. Even under His most excruciating suffering, their closeness was unbroken. Jesus trusted His Father's plan for Him and ultimately for the world.

When Jesus told His disciples to pray "In my name," He was telling them and us to do the same. We are to make it clear to our Father that above our personal desires we trust that He knows what is best for us.

Once Peter and John were on their way to the temple to pray when a beggar, lame from birth, asked them for money. Seeing the beggar's deeper need, Peter said to him, "I don't have any silver or gold for you. But I'll give you what I have. In the name of Jesus Christ the Nazarene, get up and walk!" (Acts 3:6 NLT). All the beggar asked for was money, instead he received a far better gift—an unimaginable gift, his lifelong desire to walk. Let's remember, what we ask for might not be what God knows is best for us in the long run. God might have something greater in His mind for us.

In 1987, John O'Leary, of St. Louis, Missouri, was only nine when he was playing with gasoline and created a massive explosion in his home. It burned 100% of his body. Doctors gave him a 1% chance to live. But after much prayer, numerous painful surgeries, and years of rehab, John became more than a survivor. He simply asked God to heal him and give him his life back again.

O'Leary's parents' book, *Overwhelming Odds*, tells his epic story of more than survival. For a long time after John left the hospital, he was unable to speak. Eventually he told his story to a group of third-grade Girl Scouts. Only three were present, but the telling of his story was enough to get him started.

Now, twenty years later John has spoken to millions across 49 states and in many countries. His book *In Awe* was a #1 national bestseller, and his life story will be released as a movie. So, pause and ask yourself this question? What can God do with me when I trust Him with my wounded life and ask Him, in Jesus's name, to do what He wills? John O'Leary only asked God to heal him and allow him to live, but God gave him not only his life back but opportunities to minister and reach millions of people with his story.

When Jesus says, "Ask me for anything in my name, and I will do it," it is not a magical formula for getting whatever we want. It's an invitation for us to have a trusting relationship with Him, a relationship where our desires are aligned with His desires, where we trust Him to know and do what's best for us even when we don't see it at the moment.

Could it be that God wants to give you more than what you're asking for? He just might be preparing to give you something much better than you could have imagined. Could His answer be something that will bless you, fulfill your purpose, and be a blessing to others? Keep asking, keep seeking, keep knocking, and trust that He's got something amazing in store for you when you ask, "In Jesus's name."

## FROM GOD'S WORD

(Jesus said) My purpose is to give them a rich and satisfying life.

(John 10:10 NLT)

Don't copy the behavior and customs of this world, but let God transform you into a new person by changing the way you think. Then you will learn to know God's will for you, which is good and pleasing and perfect.

(Romans 12:2 NLT)

Examine yourselves to see if your faith is genuine. Test yourselves.

(2 Corinthians 13:5 NLT)

## YOUR PRAYER

Dear Father, thank You for the precious gift of prayer. Thank You that in Your love and compassion for me, I know that You want what is ultimately best for my life and my growing relationship to You. Forgive me for my self-centeredness and for my pride. Help me to always trust You and want what You want for my life. In Jesus's name, AMEN.

## 24. A THORN IN MY SOLE

RECENTLY I WAS LOOKING THROUGH ONE of our old photo albums Mama had made when I was just a lad. Those washed-out photos sent me straight back to my second-grade self. One of the photos reminded me of a time when I had a painful experience with a thorn. Amazing are the lasting lessons that can be hidden in a pair of black, lace-up, high-top sneakers. The memory turned out to be more than a story about a thorn in my *sole*, but also about a thorn in my *soul*.

I grew up in south Florida where we lived in an old rent house next to a thickly wooded field of pine trees, palmetto bushes, and cactus plants with long, sharp thorns. It was as if those cactuses were in hiding, just waiting to prick some unsuspecting boy who wasn't watching where he was playing. One day after school, as a curious second grader, I took off running into those woods to see what I could find. I was happily unaware of the prickly cactus hiding in the underbrush until it was too late. I ran right across one, and one of its long thorns pierced all the way through my high-top sneakers, deep into my foot. The pain was excruciating, and I hobbled home, tears streaming down my face.

When Mama saw me, she came running. As she always did when I got into some mess, she held me close, comforting me as best she could. As usual, Mama was brutally honest with me. She assured me that there was no way she could remove that thorn without pulling the sneaker off. She also assured me that it was going to hurt, maybe even a lot. Again, as usual, Mama wasn't wrong.

As Mama pulled, I gritted my teeth, let out a scream, and cried. Then I noticed she was crying too. When the shoe was finally off and the thorn removed, through my tears, I asked her, "Why are you crying, Mama? I'm the one with the thorn in my foot!" I've never forgotten her words. Mama said, "When my baby boy hurts, I hurt too."

Decades later, that experience still keeps on reminding me of some profound lessons about pain, suffering, and the nature of love. Mama's tears taught me that when we genuinely love someone, their pain becomes our pain. Our suffering becomes their suffering.

That's the way it is with our Lord. The deep, empathetic love that Jesus has for us no matter what we are going through is seen throughout His life story. Isaiah 53:4-5 reminds us that Jesus took on our weaknesses and sorrows, bearing the weight of our sins. His suffering was not for His own sake but for ours. Just as Mama's heart ached with mine, Jesus's heart aches with ours in our times of suffering.

The love and care my Mama showed me gave me the strength to endure the pain, knowing she was enduring pain too. In the same way, knowing that Jesus loves us, feels our pain, and is with us through every difficulty gives us the courage to face our own thorns. Hebrews 13:5 (NLT) assures us, "I will never fail you. I will never abandon you." We are never alone in our suffering.

Don't you think that some of our pains and difficulties are like a thorn in our souls? The thorn is not of our own making, nevertheless, the misery gets our attention. We must deal with those thorns by being patient and doing what we need to do to get through the experience. But it is true that some of our pains will never go away, and we must discover God's ways of dealing with them in a productive and meaningful way. We know from Scripture that God does not always remove the thorns as it was with the Apostle Paul's thorn in the flesh.

Other times, the thorn is of our own making, as it was when I was running carelessly and the thorn pierced my foot. Although it was pain like I had not experienced, the removal of that thorn from my foot was necessary for healing. Similarly, God, in His wisdom, sometimes allows us to experience pain and hardships to bring about a greater healing in our lives. Romans 8:28 (NLT) says, "And we know that God causes everything to work together for the good of those who love God and are called according to his purpose for them." Our pain is not without purpose; it is part of the process of our restoration and growth.

Perhaps our own pain makes us more sensitive and sympathetic with others who are dealing with thorns. As Christians, we are called to share in each other's burdens. Our Heavenly Father instructs us to, "Share each other's burdens, and in this way obey the law of Christ" (Galatians 6:2 NLT). Jesus's example continues to be a great motivation for me. When I see someone hurting, it makes me want to follow His example and be His helping hand, to be His tool for compassion and action, offering comfort and support just as Mama did for me.

The thorn that pierced the sole of my shoe and my foot taught me a few lessons about other soul-piercing thorns. I realize that my pain and Mama's love are somehow mysteriously intertwined into something God has used to remind me for years that Jesus's heart aches for and with ours. He is weeping with us, carrying us, and leading us toward healing, and growing closer to Him and others.

Will you let this be a reminder that every painful crisis you experience on your journey can cause you to move forward in faith? And will you pause often to remember His ever-present love that remains steadfast, guiding you through your pain toward a greater sense of peace, purpose and hope—plus a deeper empathy for those around you?

### FROM GOD'S WORD

Share each other's burdens, and in this way obey the law of Christ.

(Galatians 6:2 NLT)

Yet it was our weaknesses he carried; it was our sorrows that weighed him down. And we thought his troubles were a punishment from God, a punishment for his own sins! But he was pierced for our rebellion, crushed for our sins. He was beaten so we could be whole. He was whipped so we could be healed.

(Isaiah 53:4-5 NLT)

## YOUR PRAYER

Father, thank You for the lessons You have taught me about my painful experiences. Help me to remember that in my pain, You are still always with me, sharing my hurts and providing the strength I need to endure whatever I must face. Help me find comfort in Your presence, guidance in Your purpose, and gratitude in Your eternal peace and hope. AMEN.

## 25. GOD'S BOOMERANG EFFECT

THE BIBLE MAKES IT OBVIOUS THAT blessing folks is part of God's nature. The first thing God did after creating His first humans was to bless them. The Bible says, "Then God blessed them" (Genesis 1:28 NLT). From the beginning to the end of the Bible, God blesses individuals. For example, the Bible says God blessed Noah (Genesis 9:1), Abraham (Genesis 12:2), Sarah (Genesis 17:16), Isaac (Genesis 26:12), Jacob (Genesis 32:29), Moses (Deuteronomy 33:1), Hannah (1 Samuel 2:21), and that's just the start. The list goes on with over six hundred references.

And Jesus was the same as His Father. In Jesus's famous Sermon on the Mount, the first word of each of His eight sermon points was the word *blessed* (Matthew 5:3-11 NLT). It's clear, if we want to be like our Creator and our Savior, one of our top goals in life must be the same—to do our best to be a blessing even when life gets tough.

But it's not easy to think about blessing others when we're immersed in our own miseries, attempting to dodge those unpredicted curveballs life throws at us. You or someone you love may be struggling right now with painful, unanticipated difficulties. But I've learned a powerful principle in the Bible that helps me see those curveballs in a whole new way. Jesus says, "Give, and you will receive. Your gift will return to you in full—pressed down, shaken together to make room for more, running over, and poured into your lap" (Luke 6:38 NLT).

At first, this principle may not seem to make sense, but over the centuries, many of us Jesus followers have found His blessing principle to be absolutely true. When we give a blessing to others while in our hardship, that's often exactly when God's *boomerang effect* kicks in. Those blessings we give others come circling back to us in surprising ways. But, in trying to bless others, I came to a better understanding of the biblical meaning of the word *bless*.

The Hebrew word for blessing is *barak*. The original root idea of blessing someone was the picture of a homeowner standing with his arms open wide at his front door, his arms graciously welcoming a needy and kneeling stranger before him. Blessing someone is about having that same attitude and doing those same kinds of acts. It's welcoming someone into your heart, your care, or gifting them with whatever God has blessed you with. It's accepting, not ignoring. It's encouraging or showing someone favor.

The image of this welcoming homeowner reminds me of one of my favorite Old Testament stories about an elderly Shunamite woman. Her story is a perfect illustration of God's boomerang effect. The Shunamite woman observed Elisha, a man of God on his missionary journeys, passing through Shunem. Although the tiny village of Shunem was on a busy trade route in Israel's Valley of Jezreel, it had no inn for travelers, and Elisha had no place to rest.

After her husband agreed, the Shunamite woman converted their attic into a small bedroom with a bed, table, lamp, and chair. The next time Elisha came by, she welcomed him into their home and invited him to stay in the special room she had made for him. For years, churches and homeowners have provided free such rooms for God's traveling missionaries. These humble rooms are often called "Prophet's Chambers" in honor of the gracious act of the Shunamite woman.

Elisha, moved by her blessing of kindness, wanted to bless her in return. When he found out she had always wanted a child, Elisha promised God would look upon her barrenness and bless her with a child. Despite her initial disbelief, she was blessed with a baby boy. But the story didn't end there. Her son grew up, became ill and died. Instead of giving up, she remembered the miracle of God's blessing through Elisha and sought him out. When she pleaded with him to ask God for a second blessing, Elisha prayed, and the boy returned to life. The Shunamite woman's story has been a reminder and encouragement for all of us that her humble blessing of Elisha by opening her home to him led to her receiving amazing blessings. They were blessings from God she never expected and were far greater than her simple sacrifices.

So how do we go about blessing someone, especially when we're battling with our own problems? Of course, there are many ways. But one of the most impactful ways that may not seem that valuable at the time is to speak an encouraging word like Jesus would.

In Peter Lord's book *Bless and Be Blessed*, he talks about the power of a simple word of encouragement. Even when you say something as simple as "I'm here for you," or "I'll be praying for you," or "You can do this," it may not feel like what you're saying means much at the time. But the truth is, God's Spirit can use your simplest heartfelt words to be an unbelievably wonderful blessing to that over-worked nurse, that bedridden friend, that worried-looking woman in the checkout line, or any number of others.

The Bible urges us to "encourage one another daily" (Hebrews 3:13 NIV). Whether someone's making a tough decision, dealing with a loss, or feeling overwhelmed, a few uplifting words can change their entire day—or even their life. Trying to be a blessing to someone who's hurting reminds me of that old Ira Wilson hymn "Make Me a Blessing," and it still rings true:

> Out in the highways and byways of life /
> Many are weary and sad.
> Carry the sunshine where darkness is rife /
> Making the sorrowing glad.
> Make me a blessing / Make me a blessing /
> Out of my life may Jesus shine;
> Make me a blessing, O Savior, I pray. Make me a blessing to someone today."

What if we made that hymn our daily prayer even when we are struggling ourselves? Our Lord teaches us over and over again that, just like the Shunamite woman, we can bless others in simple, yet profound ways. Blessing someone does not have to be by grand gestures. Sometimes, the littlest things make the biggest impact.

So next time you're facing a tough situation, remember the Shunamite woman. And in doing so, you might not only get to see God blessing others, you just might get to experience God's *boomerang effect*.

## FROM GOD'S WORD

Give, and you will receive. Your gift will return to you in full—pressed down, shaken together to make room for more, running over, and poured into your lap. The amount you give will determine the amount you get back.

(Luke 6:38 NLT)

Don't repay evil for evil. Don't retaliate with insults when people insult you. Instead, pay them back with a blessing. That is what God has called you to do, and he will grant you his blessing.

(1 Peter 3:9 NLT)

One day some parents brought their children to Jesus so… he placed his hands on their heads and blessed them.

(Matthew 19:13-15 NLT)

## YOUR PRAYER

Dear Father, when I think about how many blessings I have received from You, I am sorry I have ignored listening to Your Spirit speak to my mind and heart. I realize now that I could've been used by You to be a blessing to so many others. Even when I'm going through some hard times, help me Lord be more sensitive to the needs of other hurting people around me. It's my heartfelt desire to serve You and to be a blessing to Your children. AMEN.

## 26. AMERICA'S SURPRISING NEW EPIDEMIC

YEARS AGO, I WAS A PASTOR in Midlothian, Texas, a small town outside Dallas. Practically every morning during those nine years, I read my favorite parts of Texas's largest daily newspaper, the *Dallas Morning News*. I especially enjoyed reading the paper's popular advice columnist's daily article. I've never forgotten one particular story that included a letter from an extremely lonely woman. I'll call her Fran.

At the time she wrote her letter, Fran's husband, Tom, had completely lost his memory. Because of Tom's Alzheimer's, Fran felt alone as she helplessly watched Tom's life slowly slipping away. In her letter she pleaded for help. Fran felt so lonely and realized she was becoming deeply depressed. She often reminisced about her home, once filled with laughter and love, and now it was smothering her with a blanket of silence and isolation.

Loneliness is nothing to brush off as a weakness or something insignificant. It can actually be painful, depressing, and even unhealthy, and it is a problem most of us wrestle with at times. The circumstances that seem to trigger your feelings of loneliness may not be like Fran's. They may be from the loss of a loved one, the death of a family member or friend, a divorce or breakup, a serious illness or disability, or some other major life change.

Although loneliness has never been a stranger to humans, it appears to be increasing at a rapid pace in our country. Some behavioral and healthcare professionals are actually calling it America's new epidemic. How can America be considered "The Land of Plenty and Play" and at the same time be "The Land of Loneliness"?

Gallup Poll's recent study on loneliness reported that 61% of us feel extremely lonely sometime during the week. In 2023, the U.S. Surgeon General, Vivek Murthy, issued a national advisory warning of the potentially dangerous side effects of loneliness.

Loneliness comes in different forms and at different levels of seriousness. Of course, not all feelings of being lonely are dangerous, but any form that is prolonged can have harmful consequences. Nirappil, a health reporter for *The*

*Washington Post*, reports prolonged depression increases the risk of unhealthy depression, cognitive decline, cardiovascular issues, and even death.

Serious loneliness affects people of all age groups. According to that same Gallup Poll, young people, supposedly America's supposed most playful and happy age group, spend an average of 4.8 hours per day on social media seeking to stay in touch with their so-called friends. And yet, the same study reveals an astonishing and sad end result. They are the loneliest age group in the country and have the highest rate of suicides.

It's fair to say, you can feel lonely with a thousand Facebook friends or like Fran, sitting alone in a room with your uncommunicative husband. But pay close attention: If you feel lonely most of the time and keep saying to yourself things like, "I'm all alone. I have nobody. No one cares about me," it's time for you to make some changes.

The good news is there are several simple things you can do to help. If you're careful, you can find some highly reputable on-line medical, psychological, behavioral, and faith-based people who provide excellent counsel.

However, I want to concentrate on a resource that's available to you right now. And it's been highly effective in helping millions of people struggling with loneliness. And by the way, it's been invaluable for me personally.

Our Creator-God created us for relationship with Him and with each other. When our Heavenly Father created Adam, the first man, God said it simply, "It is not good for the man to be alone. I will make a helper who is just right for him" (Genesis 2:18 NLT). As independent as we may think we are, God knew better. He knew we humans would need at least one friend we could connect with and would be our helper and encourager. We all want and need that special someone we can count on to keep us from feeling alone. Without that connection, we will always be and feel incomplete.

That's exactly what the Lord has been for me, the One I could count on and the One who knows me best. And, if you're wondering what happened to Fran. Turns out, Fran found the same kind of help with her loneliness.

Fran recounted how one day when she felt lower than usual, she started looking through a well-worn Bible she had not opened for a long time. The Bible was a treasured gift from Tom. Hoping to get some solace and strength from it as she had once received from God's Word, she looked particularly to the words of Jesus. She told how one specific promise of Jesus seemed to grab her as though Jesus was speaking directly to her, "I will never leave thee nor forsake thee" (Hebrews 13:5 KJV).

Although Fran had felt for some time that she was alone on a deserted island, she started reading her Bible several times a day because of the emotional experience she had while reading Jesus's promise to her in the scriptures. Focusing on the words and passages about Jesus, her despondent spirit began to lift and was replaced by a growing sense of comfort and connection to her Lord.

As time passed, Fran's former vibrant faith and sense of being close to her Lord returned. She felt reconnected, talking with Him throughout each day as if He were an old friend. Before long, she started sharing her experience with a few of her former friends who began connecting with her regularly.

Fran discovered what so many of us Christians have learned. Even in our loneliest moments, we are really never alone. Jesus has never left us at all. He's been there all along. He's been waiting for us to reach out to Him so He could do what He wants most—to befriend us, love us, comfort us, and hold our hand whenever we're going through those despondent nights and days.

You can find what Fran and I found. Jesus can become that just-right friend for you—the One who removes your loneliness. He can become that special loving, caring friend you can talk with at all times. Like Fran, who was no longer lonely in Dallas, you can be no longer lonely anywhere you find yourself.

**FROM GOD'S WORD**

Come close to God, and God will come close to you.

(James 4:8 NLT)

(Jesus said) I will ask the Father, and he will give you another advocate to help you and be with you forever… he lives with you and will be in you. I will not leave you.

(John 14:16-18 NIV)

I am convinced that neither… height nor depth, nor anything else in all creation, will be able to separate us from the love of God that is in Christ Jesus our Lord.

(Romans 8:38-39 NIV)

## YOUR PRAYER

Dear Father, as You well know, life can get pretty hard. And often I get to feeling lonely and sorry for myself. Even in my loneliness, I know that You are always with me as You promised. But my emotions get confused sometimes. Forgive me for getting caught up in my circumstance and not staying in touch with You throughout the day. Help me be a better friend. I love You, Lord. AMEN.

## 27. THE NOT-SO-ORDINARY BARN OWL

JUST AFTER DAYBREAK ON ONE of our daily morning walks here in the Hill Country, Phyllis and I heard a deep, baritone hoo-hoo-hoo. Neither of us could locate the bird making such a mysterious, resonate sound. As amateur bird watchers, we have heard many bird songs, chirps, and calls in our area. After a few moments, I quietly asked our household's official bird expert, "What do you think that was?" To which she whispered, "No question, it's an owl."

When we got home, I did some research on owls and learned some interesting facts about these intriguing, feathered nocturnal birds. For instance, an owl can swivel its heads 270 degrees in either direction. That's almost all the way around. Another thing, owls have incredible hearing. While flying high above a grassy field, it can actually hear the sound of a field mouse scurrying through the grass.

The barn owl is often referred to as the *ordinary barn owl* to emphasize the contrast between its plain name and its extraordinary abilities. However, the thing that sets owls apart most from all other birds is their incomparable eyesight. The ordinary barn owl can not only see the smallest critters at exceptionally long distances, but it can also see better in the dark of the night than in daylight. Ornithologists tell us that the owl's amazing night vision is 100 times better than ours. Turns out, the so-called *ordinary* barn owl is not so ordinary after all.

Because of their unique ability to see what most of God's creatures cannot, owls are also called "wisdom birds." This reputation goes all the way back to Ancient Greece, where the owl was a symbol of Athena, the goddess of wisdom. Their keen sight and ability to navigate through darkness made them symbols of wisdom and discernment across diverse cultures and religions. Writers and artists have long used owls as symbols for the valuable connection between insight, foresight, and especially deeper spiritual truths.

Jesus often scolded arrogant religious leaders because they didn't see beyond the surface of things. He would say things like, "You have eyes but you cannot see." One of His major concerns was that those who were supposed to be the people's spiritual leaders were regretfully spiritually blind, having little understanding or interest in the spiritual values beneath the superficial. He was constantly battling spiritual blindness among prideful religious leaders.

One of His favorite idioms appearing throughout the Gospels was, "You have eyes but cannot see." For example, Mark reports Jesus asking the question, "Are your hearts too hard to take it in? You have eyes—can't you see?" (Mark 8:17-18 NLT)

The main lesson Jesus sought to convey to us through this typically symbolic phrase was that the ability to find spiritual truths and to handle our toughest circumstances comes only to us when we look beyond the surface.

In our darkest, most confusing times, it's crucial to seek to see things from God's perspective, much like the ordinary barn owl sees in the dark—seeing things most people don't even attempt to visualize. It's during these hard-hitting times that we need to open our spiritual eyes as wide as we can and seek to see through our darkness for what gift God has waiting for us.

Maybe you're living in a dark place these days—a big loss, a tough decision, or a season of uncertainty. Believe me, I know it's easy to feel overwhelmed and difficult to believe that any good could come from what you're going through. Yet, just as God created the barn owl to see in the darkness, He created you as a living soul, with special eyes too—eyes to see more than the physical. He made you with soulful, spiritual eyes to see the more in life. But here's the thing, we have to learn to use our spiritual eyes. It doesn't come naturally.

Jesus wants the best for us, even in our dark days when seeing and understanding are difficult. It takes effort and desire, but with the Spirit of God's help, we can develop this God-given, spiritual sight. When we do, we gain a new awareness of the truths and spiritual gifts He has for us. We find new courage to try things for God that we would not have tried if we only trusted in our physical eyes. This is not a quick fix. It's a gradual process—a journey of growing closer to God and learning to trust His guiding presence.

The Bible is filled with promises that God is with us in our darkest circumstances. One of my favorites is found in King David's words, "Even when I walk through the darkest valley, I will not be afraid, for you are close beside me. Your rod and your staff protect and comfort me" (Psalm 23:4 NLT).

At a glance, the ordinary barn owl may seem ordinary, but especially because of its extraordinary eyes, we know it's far from ordinary. And don't ever forget, no matter how dark you circumstances get, as one of your Father's children, you can move from ordinary to extraordinary by trusting Him through your darkness.

**FROM GOD'S WORD**

Open my eyes to see the wonderful truths in your instructions.

(Psalm 119:18 NLT)

The Lord opens the eyes of the blind. The Lord lifts up those who are weighed down.

(Psalm 146:8 NLT)

So we don't look at the troubles we can see now; rather, we fix our gaze on things that cannot be seen. For the things we see now will soon be gone, but the things we cannot see will last forever.

(2 Corinthians 4:18 NLT)

**YOUR PRAYER**

Dear Father, today, I come to You on the knees of my heart. Your Word reminds me that I am too often blind to those lessons, the people, and things You have placed right in front of me. Give me the heart and strength to follow Jesus's example so I will moment by moment see You and Your will for me, but especially in my darkest times. Thank You, Father, for seeing and listening to me. AMEN.

## 28. FROM A MEAGER SHELTER TO A MARVELOUS MANSION

HAVE YOU NOTICED HOW SOME PEOPLE transform into unrecognizable versions of themselves when a pastor enters the room? Over the years, I've observed how the way they talk, look, and even act changes. They say what they think I want to hear. They put on a smile no matter the situation or what is going on in their lives. They act happy, even when they're sad and fearful inside.

Perhaps, these folks should pay attention to King David. One reason God called King David "a man after God's own heart" (1 Samuel 13:14 NIV) was that he was not only a powerful warrior and highly revered king, but he was also a brutally honest and humble servant even with all of his problems. We can all learn an important lesson from a man like David.

David's honesty and humility got God's attention, and God moved David from the gutter of his failures to the glory of God's amazing future for him. If we want that same kind of holy second chance, even while we're still in the middle of our struggles, we must in faith patiently anticipate our Lord's intervention. When God chooses the time, He will move us as He moved David, from the shadow of our mere existence into the sunlight of His plan.

From my own struggles, I do know that it's not easy to follow David's example. Perhaps you're in the midst of a dark, difficult time. You've recently gotten some shocking news and are facing some uncertain days. You may feel like everything around you is coming apart. Maybe you or someone you love is undergoing treatment—radiation, chemo, or some other medical procedure. You may have just lost your job or worse yet, lost someone you loved dearly. Maybe you feel brutally sad, lonely, scared or confused.

Here's the question: do you think God doesn't know your heart? Do you think you need to wear a shellacked smile and pretend before Him? The Lord longs for you to do what David did, simply be honest with Him about your feelings and thoughts, be trusting of Him to reveal His future for you. He knows when you feel life has unfairly dealt you a bad hand and you see yourself as an innocent victim. He knows when you've been caught in a series of circumstances beyond your control. God is fully aware that innocent, good people have been abused, mistreated, and wounded since the beginning of humankind. But the truth God has for you is that there is real hope coming.

There is a true story tucked away in the Bible, a story that happened over 3,000 years ago. Speaking directly to these issues, it's a story of brokenness, loss, and despondency, but it's also a story of restoration, joy, and hope. It is the story of Mephibosheth (pronounced Muh-fib-uh-sheth), the story of a man who went from barely surviving in a meager shelter to thriving in a marvelous mansion.

Of course, God gave us this Bible story not to teach us that He always gives physical riches to the poor and victimized who patiently trust Him. Not at all. What He is trying to teach us is the same thing Jesus repeatedly taught the Mephibosheths of His day—that our loving and faithful Heavenly Father promises to do what He's always done for people like you and me, the unfairly treated Mephibosheths of this world. He promises that we can count on Him to graciously reward us in His surprising way—even if we're a dying thief on a cross breathing our last breath and crying out to God to remember us. God will come through.

Who was this Mephibosheth? Jews and Christians the world over are familiar with King David, Israel's most highly esteemed leader of all time. But few are familiar with his closest friend, Jonathan, the son of King Saul, Israel's first monarch. Mephibosheth was Jonathan's son.

When King Saul recognized David was rising in power and popularity among the people, the king sought to kill David and made many attempts. David and the king's son were best friends, and David promised to always take care of Saul, Jonathan, and his descendants no matter the outcome of their disputes and fighting. After the tragic deaths of King Saul and Jonathan, Mephibosheth was left alone to live as a helpless, disabled person in hiding.

When Mephibosheth's nurse learned that all of Mephibosheth's family had been killed, she quickly placed the five-year-old child in her arms and attempted to protect the child and escape danger. In fleeing, she accidentally dropped the young boy, leaving him unable to walk for the rest of his life. For years, he scarcely survived living in poverty and obscurity in a crude shelter provided by Markir, a kind, old family friend.

Growing up as a disabled and impoverished man, Mephibosheth was treated as a forgotten relic of his fallen royal family. But then, something incredible happened. What happened gives all of us who've been burdened with some undeserved adversity a renewed sense of God's hope and grace.

One ordinary day, Mephibosheth got the surprise of his life. Unbeknownst to him, God had touched king David's heart and led him to search for Mephibosheth so that he could make good on the promise he had made to Jonathan years before. David saw to it that Mephibosheth moved from meager surroundings to the King's palace. The Bible says, when Mephibosheth arrived at the palace David said, "Greetings, Mephibosheth." Mephibosheth replied, "I am your servant." "Don't be afraid!" David said. "I intend to show kindness to you because of my promise to your father, Jonathan. I will give you all the property that once belonged to your grandfather Saul, and you will eat here with me at the king's table!" (2 Samuel 9:6-7 NLT).

When you read Mephibosheth's story, you'll notice he was not supernaturally healed of his lifelong disability, but every time he bumped along on his crutches, I imagine he whispered a prayer thanking God for not giving up on him, for rescuing him when he felt forgotten and hopeless, and for the blessing of a new life of privilege with a new sense of joy, peace and purpose.

Through David's loyalty and kindness, God restored to Mephibosheth all the properties and everything else his father and grandfather had owned. Don't ever forget God has kind and selfless people out there—those whom He will send to stand up for you when you least expect it. He reassures us in His Word, "For I know the plans I have for you," says the Lord. "They are plans for good and not for disaster, to give you a future and a hope" (Jeremiah 29:11 NLT).

So, don't ever give up, and always be honest before God. God knows your heart and your needs. Keep watching for your Lord to show up like He did for Mephibosheth. Trust Him, in His perfect timing, to open the door of your meager shelter to a marvelous mansion.

### FROM GOD'S WORD

I waited patiently for the Lord to help me, and he turned to me and heard my cry. He lifted me out of the pit of despair, out of the mud and the mire. He set my feet on solid ground and steadied me as I walked along.

(Psalm 40:1-2 NLT)

We know that God causes everything to work together for the good of those who love God and are called according to his purpose for them.

(Romans 8:28 NLT)

Each time he said, "My grace is all you need. My power works best in weakness." So now I am glad to boast about my weaknesses, so that the power of Christ can work through me.

(2 Corinthians 12:9 NLT)

### YOUR PRAYER

Dear Father, sometimes, I think I have been treated unfairly. I feel like Mephibosheth—lonely, helpless, discouraged, and forgotten. But, in my heart, I know You love me and are able to help me find peace and purpose in my life. I trust You, Lord. Help me to develop the patience to wait on You to show me what I am to do with my life. Thank You for never forgetting about me. AMEN.

## 29. THE PREACHER'S COMING

MAMA WAS A SOUTHERN BELLE. Appearances mattered a great deal to Mama. Normally, she was a laid-back, fun-loving, and give-me-a-big-hug kind of a woman. But everything changed when she hung up the phone and shouted, "The preacher's coming!"

That's when Mama suddenly became the no-nonsense, drill instructor. She put on her Sunday-best dress and gave us four kids our marching orders. "Put up last night's card game, clean up your messy bedrooms, and help me straighten up that disastrous looking living room. Before he gets here, hurry up and change clothes, and get to the couch. Sit up straight and look like the perfectly behaved children you are not."

When the preacher arrived and asked Mama how she was doing, with a polite smile, she always answered the same way, "I'm fine." You see, that's what a Southern Belle does. It didn't matter if she was worried that she couldn't pay the extra medical bills, that she was having to work two jobs, that her elderly mother had moved in because she was dying from cancer, and that her husband was away much of the time for his job. She was left alone to cook three meals a day for their four kids. She was stressed out almost to her limit from responsibilities of the finances and household chores while getting ready to go to her two jobs. But "I'm fine" is what Mama said because that's what Southern Belles do.

Could it be, you're a little guilty of the same? When someone asks how you're doing, have you ever plastered on a smile and said, "I'm fine," even when you're anything but fine? Why do we do that? How can we stop living that way and be honest about how we really feel? Let's take a close look at this "I'm fine" syndrome.

Saying, "I'm fine," is something we all do. But what most people don't know is that it can take a toll on us emotionally, relationally, and even physically. When we bottle-up our emotions, we create a smokescreen to hide our true selves. We're afraid of what others might think if they knew the real us—our struggles, our messes, and our stresses. We end up suppressing our true feelings, seeing ourselves as a dishonest person, and pretending everything is okay. This isn't just a harmless habit; it's like putting a Band-Aid on an open, oozing wound that needs stitches. This facade keeps us from being the genuine Christians we aspire to be because it prevents us from opening up and releasing all those toxic feelings.

Keeping our feelings under wraps doesn't make them go away. In fact, it leads to bigger problems. It's a medical fact that hidden emotions stuffed deep inside us later present themselves as anxiety, depression, or other mental health issues. It can even affect our physical health, leading to aches, pains, sleepless nights, and more serious conditions like heart problems.

Suppressing our emotions can also cause us to feel a disconnection, a sense of being confused about our authentic selves and who we pretend to be. It also typically ends up producing strains in our relationships with those we love, and with God.

So how do you break this cycle of saying "I'm fine" when you feel like you're in a pressure cooker on the verge of exploding? This is where venting comes into play.

When the Bible writers say you need to vent, they say it this way, you need to *pour out your heart*. Wise King Solomon talked about venting in this way, "Rise during the night and cry out. *Pour out your hearts* like water to the Lord" (Lamentations 2:19 NLT). Many of our Lord's leaders encouraged their people to practice venting, pouring out their hearts when they were under pressure. David vented when he was at his wits end, "O my people, trust in him at all times. *Pour out your heart* to him, for God is our refuge" (Psalm 62:8 NLT).

Venting is more than just letting off steam. It's about sharing our feelings, frustrations, and thoughts with the Lord and with at least one other person who cares for you—a person you trust. Venting can be extremely helpful for a variety of reasons but is especially helpful in providing us needed empathy, reducing stress, finding solutions to our problems, and gaining new perspectives about our situation.

There's no shame in needing to vent! Everyone needs an outlet from time to time. In fact, studies have shown that people who regularly and honestly share their negative feelings are generally healthier than those who suppress them.

In the Bible, we see many examples of people hiding from God, suppressing their true feelings. Adam and Eve hid from God after they sinned (Genesis 3:8-10). James 1:22 talks about self-deception, where people refuse to acknowledge the truth about themselves. Hebrews 3:13 warns against self-deception, where we try to hide those times when we miss the mark that God has set for us and we only make our hearts harder and colder.

True transformation begins when we stop hiding emotionally and start opening up emotionally. Try being genuine with God and with another person by confessing, which is the Bible word for *agreeing with God* about what He already knows about us.

The highly respected theologian and writer, Richard Foster, wrote about the importance of opening up or confessing to God and others, "We tend to deny, repress, or blame others rather than owning up to our sin. But the freedom and forgiveness we crave come only as we confess our wrongdoing."

Be careful, we're not talking about self-condemnation or self-criticism but about experiencing a self-affirming transformation to a feeling of hope and freedom.

God wants the best for you. He loves you so much that He wants to be closer to you, to forgive you, and help you open up to the healthier and happier life you want, not because you've earned it, but because He is love. He's simply that way, and you're His most loved part of His creation.

Why not give up your old "I'm fine" self, and try being your new Christ-like self, your original God-designed self, your free, God-intended self.

When you do, I promise your Lord will help you, and all your relationships will become richer, more stable, and more enjoyable, even when the preacher is coming.

## FROM GOD'S WORD

The Lord hears his people when they call to him for help. He rescues them from all their troubles. The Lord is close to the brokenhearted; he rescues those whose spirits are crushed.

(Psalm 34:17-18 NLT)

Give all your worries and cares to God, for he cares about you."

(1 Peter 5:7 NLT)

Finally I confessed all my sins to you and stopped trying to hide my guilt. I said to myself, 'I will confess my rebellion to the Lord.' And you forgave me! All my guilt is gone.

(Psalm 32:5 NLT)

## YOUR PRAYER

Dear Father, forgive me for the times I put on a façade, attempting to hide my true feelings from You and my family members. I know it's not good for maintaining open, honest relationships, and I know it's not healthy for me. I know it secretly makes me see myself as a dishonest person, and I am sure You do too. Help me stop bottling-up my emotions but to be honest emotionally with You and my close friend or confidant so that I will be closer to You and more like Jesus. Please guide me as I seek to be and do all You want me to. AMEN.

## 30. ARE YOU MISSING THE SIGNS WHILE WAITING FOR THE WONDERS?

TERRY HERBERT, A METAL DETECTOR ENTHUSIAST from England, spent years scanning fields and parks all over the United Kingdom for hidden treasures. Terry was consumed with his hobby, but all he ever found were old, worthless coins and bits of metal.

Then, in 2009, he decided to explore an area near his home in Staffordshire, a place he walked practically every day. Almost immediately, his detector started beeping wildly. As he dug, he unearthed an unusual gold item. Excited, he kept digging, finding more and more gold and silver pieces.

After Terry got the university archaeologists involved, they discovered over 3,500 gold and silver artifacts from England's Anglo-Saxon period. The collection, known as the Staffordshire Hoard, is the most valuable collection of Anglo-Saxon pieces ever found.

Terry's story reminds us that the treasures we seek most are sometimes closer than we think. Terry never expected to find anything so valuable right in his every day, walking-around neighborhood.

When I first read this story, it reminded me of something Phyllis wrote in her devotional book, *Sacred Sense: From a Second Look, Volume 1.* "God's presence is experienced in the present, so learn to be mindful in the moment. Don't wait for burning bushes and flashes of light. Stop waiting and wishing for the miraculous and begin witnessing God's presence in the ordinary by taking a second look."

Sure, I'm a proud husband, so maybe I'm somewhat prejudiced, but I believe Phyllis's words are right on target. If we want to experience God's presence in our ordinary, everyday lives and be drawn closer to our Lord, we must stop waiting for burning bushes and flashes of light. Let's face it, most of us will never experience such spectacular wonders. But all of us can experience God's continual non-spectacular gifts of signs that let us know He is present with us.

We all crave the extraordinary burning bushes and flashing lights we call miracles. But it's critical to remember that the term *miracle*, as found in modern Bibles, was not present in the original

Hebrew and Greek texts. Instead, there were two Hebrew words used to describe how God revealed Himself—translated *signs* and *wonders*.

*Signs* were subtle, everyday acts of God using ordinary parts of creation to show His presence in undeniable ways. These signs served as signals or messages to His people, like the rainbow God sent as a sign of His promise: "I have placed my rainbow in the clouds. It is the sign of my covenant with you and with all the earth" (Genesis 9:13 NLT).

*Wonders*, in contrast, were spectacular acts that left people in awe of God's power. They were events so remarkable that they emphasized God's indescribable might, like Moses's Red Sea experience. "Moses raised his hand over the sea, and the Lord opened up a path through the water with a strong east wind. The wind blew all that night, turning the seabed into dry land. So, the people of Israel walked through the middle of the sea on dry ground, with walls of water on each side!" (Exodus 14:21-22 NLT).

When the Hebrew scriptures were first translated into Greek, the distinct words for *signs* and *wonders* maintained their unique meanings. However, as the Roman Empire rose and Latin became the church's official language, translators produced the Vulgate. In this Latin Bible, the two words were replaced by the single term *miraculum*, which implies something spectacular or awe-inspiring. Following this, many translations adopted this practice, leading to the modern-day interpretation of miracles as solely spectacular events.

Subsequently, in the absence of some unexplainable, breathtaking events, we might mistakenly assume God is absent, indifferent, or does not exist. But we know that is not true. God does reveal Himself through both grand wonders and more often in subtle signs continually happening in our everyday lives.

It's easy for us to miss God's signs while we're eagerly waiting for His wonders. Over the past fifty years of ministry, I've noticed that it's not those who experience the *wonder* of a mountaintop experience that continue to feel God's presence when they return to the valley. They tend to look for another *wonder* to sustain them. Those who regularly recognize the gentle, God-generated sign-posts are those who keep feeling close to Him even when they must go through the darkest valleys.

That reminds me of another unforgettable story. A young, happy, dedicated Christian couple was excited about having a little boy. But sadly, their joyful excitement suddenly turned into a fearful sorrow when their pediatrician brought them the unexpected news that their newborn was critical and there was nothing anyone could do except pray for a miracle.

Immediately they began praying and asking their family and friends to join them in asking God for a miracle. Sadly, the baby's birth defects were so severe that the infant died within hours.

You might be surprised by their reaction. Sure, their hearts were shattered. Their emotions exploded with the normal weeping and waves of grief, disbelief, sadness, and questions. Who, immersed in this panic and chaos, wouldn't have these kinds of questions: Why didn't God do a miracle? Why did this happen? Did we do something wrong? Is there a God at all?

But in just a few days when their inflamed emotions had settled down a bit, I called the young mother to ask how she was doing. This time things were different. Her voice was calm when she told me how they had hoped and prayed that God would come and heal their baby, but He didn't. But, in no surprise to me, she peacefully went on to tell me, "Our baby has died and is now with Him. As He always is, God was good and is still good. He did come and He did answer our prayers just not how we wanted. But He gave us His comfort and assurance that He will be with us through all this and will eventually reveal to us what He has in mind for us in the days ahead. We are grateful."

What a miracle! Her baby had died. She had walked through her own "valley of the shadow of death" (Psalms 23:4 KJV), and still experienced our Shepherd's peace, comfort, assurance, and most of all, His presence. Her heart was broken as any mother's would be, but her faith was not broken because she recognized God's *signs*. Perhaps this was not the kind of thing we usually think of when we talk about miracles, but there was no doubt, it was a remarkably, wonderful, and unexplainable sign of His holy presence.

Is it possible the Spirit of God is already bringing comfort, peace, joy, opportunities, and people into your life, and you've assumed it was just coincidence or good luck? Could you be wrong? Could your loving, all-powerful and all-wise Lord be working behind the scenes sending you messages that He is protecting, guiding, and helping you and your loved ones? Could it be that you don't recognize them as God's *signs*?

Be honest with yourself. Are you missing the *signs* while waiting for the *wonders*?

## FROM GOD'S WORD

Jesus broke into prayer: "Thank you, Father, Lord of heaven and earth. You've concealed your ways from sophisticates and know-it-alls, but spelled them out clearly to ordinary people. Yes, Father, that's the way you like to work."

(Matthew 11:25-26 MSG)

Every word you give me is a miracle word—how could I help but obey? Break open your words, let the light shine out, let ordinary people see the meaning.

(Psalm 119:129-130 MSG)

So here's what I want you to do, God helping you: Take your everyday, ordinary life—your sleeping, eating, going-to-work, and walking-around life—and place it before God as an offering. Embracing what God does for you is the best thing you can do for him.

(Romans 12:1 MSG)

## YOUR PRAYER

Dear Father, forgive me for spending so much time trying to convince You to do what I think You should do instead of trusting You to do what is best. Forgive me for being so arrogant in ignoring who You are and how much You love me and how You want me to experience You. Help me, Lord, to spend more of the time You've given me thanking You and looking for the many ordinary ways You show me that You are present and caring for me throughout my days. AMEN.

# ABOUT THE AUTHOR

BILL'S MISSION STATEMENT GUIDES HIS LIFE and the content of this book: Helping people to reach their full potential in Christ. For decades, he has lived that as a husband, father, grandfather, pastor, seminary professor, television executive, and author.

Dr. Nichols holds a MDiv and PhD from Southwestern Baptist Theological Seminary, where he taught Christian Philosophy, Apologetics, Evangelism, and World Religions. He began his pastoral ministry and continued as senior pastor of three churches until he was called to help found ACTS (American Christian Television System), the first faith and family television network representing the nation's mainline denominations. He went on to found Kaleidoscope Television Network, the country's first cable television channel featuring health and disability programming.

Bill has received numerous television, communications, and faith-related recognitions and awards: the Barbara Jordan Award, James Brady Award, Juvenile Diabetes International Special Service Award, The Religion in American Life Board Award, and The Inter-Faith Network Council Award.

Bill is the author of four made-for-television movies, numerous Bible and discipleship booklets, and three other books: *Healthy Faith*, *Devotions for a Healthy Faith*, and *Digging Deeper*.

Bill also enjoys painting oil portraits, landscapes, and still life subjects in a classical realism style. He and his wife Phyllis live in the Texas Hill Country where they enjoy spending time with their two married daughters and three grandchildren, writing, painting, traveling, and continuing to do Kingdom work.

Website: HealthyFaith.net
Facebook: facebook.com/Bill Nichols
Twitter: twitter.com/@cslchsnmore

www.ingramcontent.com/pod-product-compliance
Lightning Source LLC
Chambersburg PA
CBHW051822090426
42736CB00011B/1613